BRIGHT NOTES

HENRY IV, PART 1 BY WILLIAM SHAKESPEARE

Intelligent Education

Nashville, Tennessee

BRIGHT NOTES: Henry IV, Part 1
www.BrightNotes.com

No part of this publication may be used or reproduced in any manner whatsoever without written permission, except in the case of brief quotations in critical articles and reviews. For permissions, contact Influence Publishers http://www.influencepublishers.com.

ISBN: 978-1-645425-60-1 (Paperback)
ISBN: 978-1-645425-61-8 (eBook)

Published in accordance with the U.S. Copyright Office Orphan Works and Mass Digitization report of the register of copyrights, June 2015.

Originally published by Monarch Press.
Joseph E. Grennen, 1964
2019 Edition published by Influence Publishers.

Interior design by Lapiz Digital Services. Cover Design by Thinkpen Designs.

Printed in the United States of America.

Library of Congress Cataloging-in-Publication Data forthcoming.
Names: Intelligent Education
Title: BRIGHT NOTES: Henry IV, Part 1
Subject: STU004000 STUDY AIDS / Book Notes

CONTENTS

1)	Introduction to William Shakespeare	1
2)	Introduction to Henry IV, Part 1	6
3)	Textual Analysis	13
	Act I	13
	Act II	37
	Act III	63
	Act IV	87
	Act V	98
4)	Character Analyses	109
5)	Critical Commentary	114
6)	Essay Questions And Answers	120
7)	Bibliography And Guide To Research Papers	124
8)	General Biography and Criticism	133

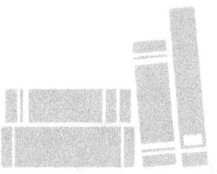

INTRODUCTION TO WILLIAM SHAKESPEARE

On April 26, 1564, William Shakespeare, son of John Shakespeare and Mary Arden, was christened in Holy Trinity Church, Stratford-on-Avon. His birthday is traditionally placed three days before. He was the eldest of four boys and two girls born to his father, a well-to-do glover and trader, who also held some minor offices in the town government. He probably attended the local free school, where he picked up the "small Latin and less Greek" that Ben Jonson credits him with. ("Small" Latin to that knowledgeable classicist meant considerably more than it does today.) As far as is known, this was the extent of Shakespeare's formal education. In November of 1582, when he was eighteen, a license was issued for his marriage to Ann Hathaway, a Stratford neighbor eight years older than himself. The following May their child Susanna was christened in the same church as her father. While it may be inferred from this that his marriage was a forced one, such an inference is not necessary; engagement at that time was a legally binding contract and was sometimes construed as allowing conjugal rights. Their union produced two more children, twins Judith and Hamnet, christened in February, 1585. Shortly thereafter Shakespeare left Stratford for a career in London. What he did during these years - until we pick him up, an established playwright, in 1592 - we do not know, as no records exist. It is presumed that he served an apprenticeship in the theatre, perhaps as a provincial trouper, and eventually won himself a place as an actor. By 1594 he was a successful dramatist with the Lord Chamberlain's company (acting groups had noble protection and patronage), having produced the *Comedy of Errors* and the *Henry VI* trilogy, probably in collaboration with older, better established dramatists. When the plague closed the London theatres for many months of 1593-94, he found himself without a livelihood. He promptly turned his hand to poetry (although written in verse, plays were not considered as dignified as poetry), writing two long narrative poems, *Venus and Adonis* and *The Rape of Lucrece*. He dedicated them to the Earl of Southampton, undoubtedly receiving some recompense. The early nineties also saw the first of Shakespeare's **sonnets** circulating in manuscript, and later finding their way into print. In his early plays - mostly chronicle histories glorifying England's past, and light comedies - Shakespeare sought for popular success and achieved it. In 1599 he was able to buy a share in the Globe Theatre, where he acted and where his plays were performed. His ever-increasing financial success enabled him to buy a good deal of real estate in his native Stratford, and by 1605 he was able to retire from acting. Shortly thereafter he began to spend most of his time in Stratford, to which he retired around 1610. Very little is known of his life after he left London. He died on April 23, 1616, in Stratford, and was buried there. In 1623 the *First Folio* edition of his complete works was published by a group of his friends as a testimonial to his memory. This was a very rare tribute, because at the time plays were generally considered to be inferior literature, not really worthy of publication. These scanty facts, together with some information about the dates of his plays, are all that is definitely known about the greatest writer in the history of English literature. The age in which Shakespeare lived was not as concerned with keeping accurate records as we are, and any further details about Shakespeare's life have been derived from educated guesses based on knowledge of his time. Shakespeare's plays fall into three major groups according to the periods in his development when he wrote them:

EARLY COMEDIES AND HISTORIES

The first group consists of romantic comedies such as *A Midsummer Night's Dream* (1593-5), and of strongly patriotic histories such as *Henry V* (1599). The early comedies are full of farce and slapstick, as well as exuberant poetry. Their plots are complicated and generally revolve around a young love relationship. The histories are typical of the robust, adventurous English patriotism of the Elizabethan era, when England had achieved a position of world dominance and power.

THE GREAT TRAGEDIES

The second period, beginning with *Hamlet* and ending with *Antony and Cleopatra*, is the period of the great tragedies: *Hamlet* (1602); *Othello* (1604); *King Lear* (1605); *Macbeth* (1606); and *Antony and Cleopatra* (1607-8). Shakespeare seems to have gone through a mental crisis at this time. His vision of the world darkens, and he sees life as an **epic** battle between the forces of good and evil, between order and chaos within man and in the whole universe. The forces for good win out in the end over evil, which is self-defeating. But the victory of the good is at great cost and often comes at the point of death. It is a moral victory, not a material one. These tragedies center on a great man who, because of some flaw in his makeup, or some error he commits, brings death and destruction down upon himself and those around him. They are generally considered the greatest of Shakespeare's plays.

THE LATE ROMANCES

In the third period Shakespeare returns to romantic comedy. But such plays as *Cymbeline* (1609-10), *The Winter's Tale* (1610-11), and *The Tempest* (1611) are very different in point of view and structure from such earlier comedies as *Much Ado About Nothing* (1599) and *Twelfth Night* (1600). Each of these late romances has a situation potentially tragic, and there is much bitterness in them. Thus the destructive force of insane jealousy serves as the **theme** both of the tragedy, *Othello*, and the comedy, *The Winter's Tale*. They are serious comedies, replacing farce and slapstick with rich symbolism and supernatural events. They deal with such **themes** as sin and redemption, death and rebirth, and the conflict between nature and society, rather than with simple romantic love. In a sense they are deeply religious, although unconnected with any church dogma. In his last play, *The Tempest*, Shakespeare achieved a more or less serene outlook upon the world after the storm and stress of his great tragedies and the so-called "dark comedies."

SHAKESPEARE'S THEATRE

Shakespeare's plays were written for a stage very different from our own. Women, for instance, were not allowed to act; so female parts, even that of Cleopatra, were played by boy actors whose voices had not yet changed. The plays were performed on a long platform surrounded by a circular, unroofed theatre, and were dependent on natural daylight for lighting. There was no curtain separating the stage from the audience, nor were there act divisions. These were added to the plays by later editors. Because the stage jutted right into the audience, Shakespeare was able to achieve a greater intimacy with his spectators than modern playwrights can. The audience in the pit, immediately surrounding the stage, had to stand crowded together throughout the play. Its members tended to be lower class Londoners who would frequently comment aloud on the action of the play and break into fights. Anyone who attended the plays in the pit did so at the risk of having his pockets picked, of catching a disease, or, at best, of being jostled about by the crude "groundlings." The aristocratic and merchant classes, who watched the plays from seats in the galleries, were spared most of the physical discomforts of the pit.

ITS ADVANTAGES

There were certain advantages, however, to such a theatre. Because complicated scenic, lighting and sound effects were impossible, the playwright had to rely on the power of his words to create scenes in the audience's imagination. The rapid changes of scene and vast distances involved in *Antony and Cleopatra*, for instance, although they create a problem for modern producers, did not for Shakespeare. Shakespeare did not rely - as the modern realistic theatre does - on elaborate stage scenery to create atmosphere and locale. For these, as for battle scenes involving large numbers of people, Shakespeare relied on the suggestive power of his poetry to quicken the imagination of his audience. Elizabethan audiences were very lively anyway, and quick to catch any kind of word play. Puns, jokes, and subtle poetic effects made a greater impression on them than on modern audiences, who are less alert to language.

INTRODUCTION TO HENRY IV, PART 1

BACKGROUND OF THE PLAY

Historical

Richard II, the only son of Edward, the Black Prince, he himself the oldest son of Edward III, came to the throne upon the death of Edward in 1377, the Black Prince having died before his father. Henry Bolingbroke, also a grandson of Edward III, was the son of John of Gaunt, Duke of Lancaster and Edward III's third son. Bolingbroke had been exiled to France by Richard, but returned when, upon the death of his father, Richard had seized the Lancastrian estates. With the aid of the Percies, a powerful northern family, Bolingbroke carried on a successful revolt, deposed Richard, and (presumably) had him murdered in 1399; he came to the throne as Henry IV. Shakespeare treats all of this in his Richard II, which is a study of kingship that has devolved upon a man who is at worst weak and at best one whose vision is poetical rather than practical. Bolingbroke was a usurper, though upon the death of Richard he might have been unquestionably the legitimate king except for one thing-a surviving male in the direct line tracing back to Edward III through his second son Lionel, Duke of Clarence. This potential claimant was Edmund Mortimer, Earl of March (Shakespeare confuses him with the Edmund

Mortimer who married the daughter of the Welsh chieftain Owen Glendower). The Percies, disillusioned with Henry, rebelled. The two forces met at the Battle of Shrewsbury (1403), and the Percies went down to defeat. There is historical warrant for other details of the story (in Holinshed's *Chronicle)*, notably Glendower's uprising, and the waywardness of the Prince.

Dramatic Traditions

a. The "History Play." History plays (or chronicle plays) were phenomena of the Elizabethan period, mainly of the years immediately following the defeat of the Spanish Armada (1588), which has led to the conjecture that the national fervor of the times was a chief cause of the plays. But it is undoubtedly also true that the general Renaissance interest in history as a broad mirror of civilization (seen in the popularity of the *Mirror for Magistrates*, a work in the medieval de casibus, or "fall of great men" tradition) had much to do with it. Certainly, the increased interest in realpolitik, of which Elyot's *The Governor* and Machiavelli's *Prince* are well-known examples, also favored their production. The nature of the history play is a complicated subject, one which has been studied at great length by Lily B. Campbell in her book Shakespeare's "Histories": *Mirrors of Elizabethan Policy*. Suffice it to say that in the so-called "Lancastrian tetralogy" (*Richard II*, the two parts of *Henry IV*, and *Henry V)* Shakespeare displays a searching interest in the nature of kingship - the personality of the ruler - and seems quite clearly to be insisting through these plays on the essential rightness of Henry Bolingbroke's seizure of the throne, both because of Richard's weakness and his own strength, and because ultimately it brought a paragon of kingliness, his son Henry, to the throne as Henry V.

b. The "Native Drama": Shakespeare's sense of structure, his handling of verse techniques, his use of dramatic devices (such as the "messenger" for reporting off-stage action), were unquestionably influenced, at least indirectly, by the sixteenth-century interest in Roman drama. The "stock characters" of Roman comedy, for one thing, tended to reappear in English plays; Falstaff, whatever else he may be, owes something to the "braggart soldier" type of the Roman comedy. But Shakespeare's deeper roots were in the native drama. It has been suggested, in fact, that *Henry IV, Part One* is really in the immediate tradition of the medieval morality play, with the young Prince (Youth) being tempted to a sinful life by Falstaff (Vanity). And there seems no doubt that Shakespeare's masterful use of the double plot (a main plot involving the actions of the "noble" characters, and a subplot which parallels the action of the main plot for emphasis, **irony**, or humor) is in a tradition reaching back to the medieval *Second Shepherds' Play* in which the birth of the divine Child is paralleled by the farcical actions of shepherds and their sheep. Needless to say, no debt to traditions of any kind begins to compare with Shakespeare's transforming genius.

BRIEF SUMMARY OF HENRY IV, PART ONE

Act I

King Henry, in council in his palace, is celebrating a momentary lull in the civil disturbances besetting the nation, and he reiterates his former intention of visiting the Holy Land. He is told that the Welsh, under Owen Glendower, have defeated Edmund Mortimer, Earl of March. This is partly offset by the fact that Harry Percy (Hotspur), fighting in the north against the Scots, has defeated Douglas and refuses to relinquish his prisoners to Henry until the King promises to ransom Mortimer.

Henry is annoyed with Hotspur, but even more annoyed with his wastrel son Hal, who could use a little of Hotspur's moxie (or so Henry thinks). The next scene shows the Prince carousing in his London apartment with Falstaff, an amiable reprobate knight, and matching wits with him. They speak of a robbery to take place the next night. Privately, Poins, another of Hal's low companions, reveals a plan to allow Falstaff and the rest of their cronies to take the purses but to set on them in disguise, return to their hangout, the Boar's Head Tavern, and wait for Falstaff to come back and tell his monstrous lies about what happened. The next scene shifts back to the palace, where the Percy group (the Earl of Northumberland, his son Hotspur and his brother Worcester) has been summoned by the King. Hotspur tries to explain that he refused the prisoners because the King sent his message through an effeminate lord who rubbed him the wrong way. We see that Hotspur is something of a choleric individual. They still refuse the prisoners, and the King threatens reprisals. Left by themselves, the Percies discuss the King's highhanded ways, and intimate strongly that he is suspicious of them because he fears they will try to overthrow him in favor of Mortimer. They decide to revolt.

Act II

The first scene shows one of the thieves, Gadshill, looking over some travelers at an inn in Rochester as prospects for the robbery. In the second scene, the robbery takes place and, as planned, the Prince and Poins steal the loot from Falstaff and the others who then run away in confusion. The third scene shifts to Hotspur at his castle; he is reading a letter from a lord who has cautiously refrained from throwing his fortune in with the rebels. His conversation with his wife reveals his essentially martial character. In the following scene, we are at

BRIGHT NOTES STUDY GUIDE

the Boar's Head Tavern where, to pass the time, the Prince and Poins are chaffing the apprentice lads, especially a "drawer" named Francis. Falstaff enters with his crew. He is loud in his condemnation of the "cowards" Hal and Poins who missed the robbery. They lead him on, and he tells a magnificent and amusing lie about the "hundred" men who attacked them and took their booty. Faced with the true facts, he pretends he knew it was the Prince all along. They turn to the subject of the King's dissatisfaction with the Prince and act out an imaginary interview between Henry and Hal (both taking each role in turn). The sheriff arrives, looking for Falstaff, and the Prince dismisses him, promising to send Falstaff to him the next day. Falstaff is discovered asleep behind a tapestry as the scene ends.

Act III

We are at Glendower's castle in Wales, where we see Hotspur arguing with Glendower, simply because the Welshman's affectations annoy him. Hotspur, Mortimer, and Glendower (with considerable quibbling by Hotspur) divide the kingdom into the three parts they will take when the revolt has been successfully carried out. The next scene moves to the King's palace and we are watching the interview between Henry and the Prince. In a long speech, Henry chides him for becoming a "companion to the common streets" like the former King Richard II. The Prince promises to reform, and Henry promises him a command. Sir Walter Blunt enters with the news that the rebels met with Douglas the Scot at Shrewsbury. We then move to the Boar's Head Tavern, where Falstaff exercises his wit at the expense of Bardolph (for his fiery red face) and the hostess until the Prince and Poins come in with the news that they are all off to the wars-Falstaff as captain of an infantry troop.

Act IV

This act begins in the rebel camp, where Hotspur and the other leaders are receiving word that Northumberland and Glendower are pulling out, the Earl because of "illness" and Glendower because he cannot muster the necessary forces in time. The rebels are somewhat disturbed, but Hotspur rallies them. This is followed by a scene showing Falstaff describing the ragged crew he has drafted into service (at a profit for himself); we then return to the rebel camp, to discover that their confidence is disintegrating. Blunt approaches with an offer of pardon if they will disband. Hotspur delivers a violent condemnation of the King but promises to think it over. A very brief scene shows the Archbishop of York (one of the conspirators) very worried about the outcome.

Act V

The scene is in the King's camp. Worcester and Sir Richard Vernon enter with the rebel's answer. They condemn the King's "lack of faith"; he offers them pardon once again, and the Prince offers to settle the issue by single combat with Hotspur. Henry refuses to allow this, and there is a brief soliloquy by Falstaff on the insubstantiality of "honor." We return to the rebel camp, where Worcester lies to Hotspur, telling him the King offered no terms. Vernon, however, does repeat the Prince's offer of single combat, and Hotspur vows to seek him out on the field. The third scene shows the battlefield, where we see Douglas kill Blunt; Falstaff enters followed by the Prince, who reaches into Sir John's pistol case only to find there a bottle of sack (wine). The next scene shows another part of the field, where the King, being bested by Douglas, is rescued by the Prince. Hotspur appears and is killed by the Prince, who makes a speech over his body extolling his valiancy, while Falstaff lies nearby where he has been playing "possum" to escape from Douglas. When the Prince leaves, Falstaff rises, stabs the dead body of Hotspur and raises it to his shoulders; he meets the Prince and his brother John and tries to convince them that he and Hotspur, down and out of breath but not dead, rose and fought it out.

The last scene of the play reveals the King, now victorious, sentencing Worcester and Vernon to death. The Prince gives Douglas his freedom, and the play ends with Henry's speech determining to do equivalent justice on Northumberland and Glendower.

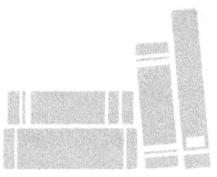

HENRY IV, PART 1

TEXTUAL ANALYSIS

ACT I

ACT I: SCENE 1

The scene opens at the royal palace in London where King Henry has assembled his courtiers, Prince John of Lancaster (his younger son), the Earl of Westmoreland, Sir Walter Blunt, and others. The purpose of the meeting is to hear Westmoreland's report on a session of the King's council, called to discuss his projected trip to the Holy Land. In measured and formal tones, Henry describes the present moment as a brief period of respite from the ravages of the civil war which has lately been raging. He calls it "the intestine shock, and furious close of civil butchery."

Comment

These words suggest the close analogy felt by the Elizabethans between the structure of the cosmos (the heavens), the state (or kingdom), and the human individual. Civil war was not merely an unfortunate opposition of political forces leading to bloodshed; it was a disruption of the very basis of society-order. It provoked disturbances in the heavens and was an attack on civil "health," as disease is an attack on bodily health.

Henry optimistically predicts a period of calm when former enemies shall become allies, giving him the opportunity of visiting the sepulchre of Christ, of organizing a crusade, in fact, to chase the infidels from the holy places.

Comment

The ambiguity of the king's position shines through his entire speech. He wishes to administer his kingdom in peace and prosperity, yet his own usurpation of the throne is the very cause of the unsettled conditions which prevail. And his decision to visit Jerusalem, while it is befitting a Christian ruler at any time, can be regarded at this precise moment as an act of expiation for the murder of Richard II, a divinely anointed king himself. The coronation of a rightful king came very close to being a sacramental act, and regicide was the most heinous of crimes.

The King asks Westmoreland for his report, and is immediately told that plans for the voyage have been postponed because word had been received that Edmund Mortimer, Earl of March, has been captured by the Welshman Owen Glendower and a thousand of his men have been butchered. What is more, the Welshwomen had performed horrible mutilations upon the dead bodies. Added to this was a report from the north country that young Henry Percy had engaged Archibald, Earl of Douglas, in combat-as yet, undecided. The King, however, has a later report from Sir Walter Blunt that Douglas has been vanquished, and several of his Scots compatriots taken prisoner by Percy. "And is not this an honorable spoil? A gallant prize?" asks Henry. To which Westmoreland thoughtlessly replies: "In faith it is a conquest for a prince to boast of."

Comment

Westmoreland's casual **simile** is taken literally by the King, who immediately begins to brood over the differences between the Earl of Northumberland's son Henry (young Percy), who is the "**theme** of honor's tongue," and "sweet fortune's minion and her pride," and his own son Prince Henry (or Hal), at the moment given over to "riot and dishonor." The whole question of honor and of the conduct befitting a prince, are major concerns of the play, and Henry's constant comparisons of the young Percy with the Prince force the audience to make the same comparisons.

The King then angrily declares that "Hotspur" (the surname of young Percy) has refused to relinquish any prisoners to the crown save Mordake, Earl of Fife. Westmoreland attributes this to the prompting of the Earl of Worcester Thomas Percy (Hotspur's uncle). Henry asserts that he has summoned Hotspur, that he has put off the Jerusalem pilgrimage, and that he will hold court at Windsor on the coming Wednesday, since there is much to be said and done.

SUMMARY

In this opening scene the following things are accomplished:

1. We are, of course, introduced to two major characters: the King himself, who we learn is unsettled in mind

and beset by broils in the west and north and by incipient treason by the northern Percies; and, Westmoreland, who is a practical politician and a man of no sentimental illusions.

2. The main plot, which involves the insurrection of the Percies, a powerful family which had been instrumental in putting Henry on the throne, is here set in motion with the report of Hotspur's refusal to yield his prisoners.

3. What will later be seen as a major action of the play-Prince Hal's failure to measure up to his father's expectations, and his subsequent reform-is here given explicit utterance.

4. Related **themes** are introduced, especially (a) the nature of "honor," and (b) the results of violating established "order."

5. Particular images, which will later be seen to belong to a pattern of **imagery** (providing an important aspect of the play's meaning), mark the speech of the characters. For example, (a) the "beastly transformation" practiced by the Welshwomen by being a form of excess or "enormity" anticipates the later enormity (both physical and moral) of Sir John Falstaff.

6. The language of this scene (poetry rather than prose) is highly figurative, rhythmical, and formal. It tends to lend formality and ceremony to the affairs of kingship, and thus suggests the gravity of the

> offense of young Prince Hal, now given over to "riot and disorder."

ACT I: SCENE 2

The scene is now the Prince of Wales' London apartment. Hal and Sir John Falstaff enter, conversing in prose.

Comment

Shakespeare's meaning is frequently to be found in the implicit comparisons which the juxtaposition of scenes and characters demands. Here, in place of his royal father's ceremonial council, we have Hal "holding court" for his low companions. Answering to Westmoreland's dignified practicality in counseling the King is Falstaff's infantile morality. (We come to understand this gradually as the play develops.) Shakespeare is not, by any means, the only Elizabethan dramatist to present his **theme** through the device of the "double plot," but he is a master of its use.

Falstaff asks the time of day, and is treated to an outburst of good-humored abuse by the Prince, who strikes the keynote of Falstaff's character by emphasizing his weakness for sack (wine), capons, and wenches-in short, the pleasures of the flesh. He tells Sir John that he ought to have no interest in the time of day, unless "hours were cups of sack" and "the blessed sun himself a fair hot wench in flame-colored taffeta." Falstaff responds on a note of false rhetoric, saying, "we that take purses go by the moon and the seven stars, and not by Phoebus [the sun], he, that wand'ring knight so fair." He calls the Prince "sweet wag" (a term of easy familiarity) and jests with Hal in a way that shows the intimacy of their friendship.

Comment

Falstaff handles language in truly virtuoso fashion. He can quip, riddle, and pun, command a high rhetorical flourish, or descend to good-natured badinage or outright abuse. Whatever might be said of his physical constitution (Hal later calls him, among other insulting enormities, "a gross mountain of a man," for instance), or his moral fibre, his speech proves that he is intellectually facile, and this fact alone gives him the right to comment on other men's tendencies to mask their motives in hypocritical formulas. This, as we later see, is one of Falstaff's many functions.

They continue their mock battle of wit, Falstaff asking the Prince, when he becomes king, to "let not us that are squires of the night's body [his band of cutpurses-with a pun on "knight"] be called thieves of the day's beauty [or "booty"]." Beneath the joking one can discern the Prince's clear understanding of their lawless life, and his realization that society will ultimately judge and punish. He appears to have a genial tolerance of Falstaff's errant ways and a fascinated attraction to the way of life he represents. But Hal never really countenances lawlessness. When Falstaff asks, "But I prithee, sweet wag, shall there be gallows standing in England when thou art king? and resolution [his kind of courage] thus fubbed as it is with the rusty curb of cold father antic the law? Do not thou, when thou art king, hang a thief," the Prince quickly promises him the hanging of thieves. Falstaff immediately takes this to mean a judgeship, but Hal tells him he is judging wrong already-he is to be the hangman.

Comment

Falstaff's indictment of "the rusty curb of old father antic the law" shows his position with respect to the order a true society demands. There is something cynical in Falstaff's attitude toward the law, just as there is something slightly hypocritical in the King's desire (now that civil war has brought him the crown) that the opposing armies cease their struggles and march in the order of "mutual well-beseeming ranks." At the moment, this is one way of looking at the Prince's problem of choosing between them. Hal has learned to parry with language in such a way that he can languish in the company of these thieving brethren without ever committing himself to their principles or being trapped into a promise to countenance them once he has become king.

Being a hangman, Falstaff replies, suits his temperament very well, for he is as melancholy as a gib cat (an altered tomcat), a baited bear, or (the Prince adds) an old lion or a lover's lute, a hare, or Moor Ditch itself (an open sewer in London). More than a mere contest in witty similes, there is here an undercurrent of reference to Falstaff as a man grown old in lechery. He draws back from the combat, saying that the Prince uses the "most unsavory similes," and asks Hal to "trouble [him] no more with vanity." The very word "vanity," the moralist's term for all the transient pleasures of the world, seems to provoke a kind of mock repentance in Falstaff; he mentions an "old lord" who recently chided him about the Prince, and they both jest (playing on biblical terminology) about Wisdom crying out in the streets and no man regarding it. With whimsical mockery, the fat knight alleges that the Prince has led him astray and climaxes this absurd accusation by expostulating: "I'll be damned for never a king's son in Christendom." Hal, refusing to be taken in by Falstaff's pretense of outraged morality, asks where they will take a purse (that is, commit thievery on the high road) on the morrow. Falstaff quickly rises to the bait and agrees to the deed wherever the Prince desires it. With some sarcasm, the Prince comments on Falstaff's "good amendment of life; from praying to purse-taking." With feigned surprise that he should be accused of sinful intentions, Falstaff offers his defense: "Why, Hal, 'tis my vocation, Hal. 'Tis no sin for a man to labor in his vocation."

At this point, Ned Poins, another cutpurse, enters, Falstaff welcomes him, knowing that he will have information about a proposed robbery, and praises him to the Prince as "the most omnipotent villain that ever cried Stand!' [in modern parlance, "Don't make a move!"] to a true man. Poins now takes up the good-natured jesting at Falstaff's expense, referring to him as "Monsieur Remorse" (for his pretended melancholy and moral reform) and as "Sir John Sack and Sugar" (for his appetites), and accuses him of selling his soul to the devil on Good Friday for a cup of wine and a cold capon's leg. The Prince then comments that the devil will have his due, for Sir John "was never yet a breaker of proverbs."

Comment

"To give the devil his due," is a proverb and proverbs after all, are statements which embody constantly recurring situations-typical human situations. Hal seems to imply by this remarks that Sir John is thoroughly representative of human nature in its widest sense - and in all its ambiguity-because any proverb at all finds an illustration in him.

Poins reveals the plot. On the next morning at four o'clock a number of rich pilgrims will be riding to Canterbury, and tradesmen will be riding to London, past Gad's Hill (apparently their favorite place for holdups-one of the cutpurses is named "Gadshill", in fact). Poins has masks for all of them and has arranged for their supper in Eastcheap (a district in London). If they will come along, their purses will be stuffed with "crowns," if not, they may stay at home and "hang them all." Falstaff asks the Prince if he will take part in the robbery. He refuses. Sir John abuses him by saying that he has "neither honesty, manhood, nor good fellowship" in him, and that he "cam'st not of the blood royal" if he dares not "stand for ten shillings."

Comment

Falstaff is punning here on the word "royal," which was a coin worth about ten shillings. This, together with Poins' remark about "stuffing their purses full of crowns," contains subdued suggestions about crowns and royalty which mirror the serious treatment of this **theme** in the main plot. It is significant that the Prince here refuses to participate. Shakespeare could hardly represent young Hal as a common thief, even if the conception had been part of his total design. But his design, in fact, seems to have been to show the Prince as fascinated by the positive attractions of Falstaff and the others-good fellowship, wit, frank acceptance of human appetite-rather than their criminal activities.

Falstaff humorously threatens to retaliate by becoming a traitor when Hal is king, but the Prince says that he does not care. Poins asks Falstaff to leave him alone with the Prince, and the knight exits. Poins then takes Hal into his confidence, revealing that he needs his participation in a jest that he cannot manage alone. They will let Falstaff, Gadshill, Bardolph, and Peto (the last two of the band of thieves) rob the travelers and, once they have the booty, set upon them in disguise and rob them in turn. They will first conceal their horses and then don buckram suits to disguise their easily recognizable clothes. The Prince expresses fear that he and Poins may not be able to overpower the other four, to which Poins replies: "Well, for two of them, I know them to be as true-bred cowards as ever turned back; and for the third, if he fight longer than he sees reason, I'll forswear arms."

Comment

The reference to the "third" seems to be a clear reference to Falstaff, and this passage first raises the issue which has become famous in criticism of the play-is Falstaff a coward or not? (This question will be treated later in more detail.) Poins, at least, seems to make a distinction between outright cowardice and that kind of resourcefulness which allows a man to "live to fight another day."

The humor of the jest, Poins goes on, will be the "incomprehensible lies" that the fat knight will tell them when they later meet at supper-how many set upon them, how valiantly he fought, and what blows he endured. In the rebuking of Sir John for his lies will be the point of the whole affair. The Prince agrees to take part. Poins leaves, and Prince Hal has the stage to himself for what has become one of the most famous of Shakespearean soliloquies.

Comment

The soliloquy was, originally simply a conventional way of allowing the Elizabethan audience some direct knowledge of what was going on in the mind of a stage character. (In modern movies this is easily handled by having the previously recorded voice of the actor dubbed into a scene in which he appears, obviously pondering, and not moving his lips.) With Shakespeare, especially in his more mature plays, one can never be sure that the soliloquy represents no more than the conscious thoughts of the character. It has even been suggested that this particular soliloquy is a kind of prologue, imparting information about Hal's future reformation to the audience, which even he does not possess. On the other hand, it is possible to make sense of the Prince's character even by assuming that his consorting with Falstaff and the others, and his ultimate rejection of them, is deliberate and calculated. Needless to say, the point is arguable.

The Prince avers that he knows his companions for what they are and will merely tolerate them for a time, just as the sun allows itself to be obscured by clouds so that its beauty will be more wondered at when it is again visible. Holidays are appreciated because they come seldom, and only "rare accidents" are pleasing. So he, when he throws off his wanton ways, something he has never given promise of doing, will shine "like bright metal on a sullen ground," and his reformation will consequently be the more admired for being unexpected.

SUMMARY

This scene generates the subplot, and specifically:

1. Introduces us to the raucous characters whose "plotting" of thievery comically mirrors the King's councils of war. Even the dissension of Poins and the Prince from the others anticipates the intramural infighting in the royalist and rebel camps.

2. It gives us a first vision of Prince Hal, who is the common factor between the two plots, and it provides us with a glimpse at his understanding of the problem of the relative claims of personal desire and kingly self-abnegation.

3. It introduces Falstaff, a character who is at last as important as the Prince (some feel, more important) to the total meaning of the play, and it gives us a concrete sampling of his wit and moral stance and the regard in which he is held by the Prince and Poins. His enormous size (later brought out in the humor of outrageous insult) is here only vaguely alluded to.

4. By jest, subtle word-play, and quibble, as well as by action, it carries on the **themes** (introduced in Scene 1) of "honor," "order," "kingship," and "reformation."

5. Through the Prince's soliloquy (whether he is conscious of it or not) we are explicitly reminded that he does eventually overcome whatever attraction Falstaff's crew had for him.

ACT I: SCENE 3

The scene is London, the King's palace. The King enters with Sir Walter Blunt and other courtiers, as do the elder Percy (the Earl of Northumberland), his son Henry Percy (Hotspur), and his brother Thomas Percy (Earl of Worcester). The King speaks-in a formal, cold, even overbearing manner-alleging that his blood has been too temperate (that is, his anger too slow to rise) and his patience too long-suffering, considering the indignities the Percies have heaped upon him. He promises to be mighty in the future and feared, rather than smooth and soft and lacking respect as in the past. Worcester demurs mildly, asserting that their house, which has helped Henry to the throne, little deserves to have that very power used against it so ruthlessly.

Comment

Without the Percies' help, Henry Bolingbroke (formerly Duke of Hereford, and banished from England by Richard II) would not have been able to wage a successful revolt against Richard. (This banishment and revolt, the murder of Richard, and the accession of Henry, make up the main action of Shakespeare's *Richard II*.)

The King angrily dismisses Worcester, calling his manner bold and peremptory, and informs him that he will send for him when he needs his counsel.

Comment

Worcester's tone of address is far from "peremptory," and we begin to feel that some hidden suspicion motivates Henry's charge.

The King then turns to the Earl of Northumberland, who in turn tries to mitigate Henry's wrath by explaining that young Harry's (Hotspur's) denial of the King's demand for the prisoners was not couched in the strong terms which have apparently been reported to him. Either envy or misunderstanding is at the root of the matter, he affirms.

Hotspur then depends himself in a long, impressive, and vivid account of the circumstances under which the King's demand was presented to him. It was on the battlefield, and he was "breathless and faint, leaning on his sword." A lord, the King's messenger, impeccably dressed, shaven and scented, and carrying a dainty perfume box, came smiling and talking even while the dead bodies were being carried from the field. He called them "unmannerly" to bring a "slovenly unhandsome corse" between him and the wind. With many "holiday and lady terms" he demanded the prisoners. Hotspur smarting from his wounds, was infuriated at this "popinjay" and made some negligent answer. He was maddened by this "waiting gentlewoman" with his talk about the virtues of spermaceti for internal injuries, and the "great pity" it was that "this villainous saltpetre [for gunpowder] should be digged out of the harmless earth." Except for these "vile guns" he would have been a soldier himself. Hotspur, finally, implores the King not to let the report of such a namby-pamby be the occasion of their estrangement.

Comment

The King does not gainsay the account Hotspur gives, nor is it vital to the action of the play in any case. The description of this foppish and effeminate lord is far more important as an underscoring of Hotspur's virile courage and contempt for cowardice than as a believable **exposition** of the actual event on the battlefield.

Even Sir Walter Blunt, of the King's party, beseeches Henry to let sleeping dogs lie if young Percy is willing to make amends at this time. But the King reveals that Hotspur still refuses him the prisoners, except on condition that he ransom Hotspur's brother-in-law Edmund Mortimer, Earl of March, who the King says has "willfully betrayed the lives of those that he did lead to fight against that great magician, damned Glendower."

Comment

This "betrayal" was Mortimer's marriage with the daughter of Owen Glendower, the Welsh chieftain. Henry also seems to be in the grip of a superstitious fear of Glendower's reputed abilities in magic. The whole question of magic, real or mock (as in Falstaff's later "resurrection" from the dead), is a minor motif in the play.

Henry, in any case, refuses to ransom a man he believes to be a traitor and in unequivocal terms gives his opinion of the Earl of March: "I shall never hold that man my friend / Whose tongue shall ask me for one penny cost / To ransom home revolted Mortimer."

Hotspur picks up the King's term, "revolted Mortimer," and in an impassioned outburst, attempts to defend Mortimer's actions before the King. Mortimer, he declares, never gave less than full loyal support to the King, except through the accidents of war. It takes only one tongue to describe the many "mouthed wounds" which he received on the bank of the Severn while he spent the greater part of an hour in single combat with the great Glendower.

Comment

"Mouthed wounds" means slashes in the flesh resembling mouths (and note the play on "tongue" and "mouth"). The best poetry of the play is given to Hotspur, though he frequently bursts out with a high rhetorical flourish. This speech, in any event, is one of Hotspur's finest pieces of rhetoric.

> "Three times they breathed, and three times did they drink, Upon agreement, of swift Severn's flood, Who then, affrighted with their bloody looks, Ran fearfully among the trembling reeds And hid his crisp head in the hollow bank, Bloodstained with these valiant combatants."

The very excess of imagination which the subject of combat and glory calls forth from Hotspur is itself a qualification of the point of view he represents. But it is undoubtedly going too far to see in young Percy's glamorizing of the miseries of battle a subtle attack by Shakespeare on the horrors of war (an idea which has, in fact, been suggested).

Dissimulation (if that is what the King imputes to Mortimer, Hotspur implies) never worked with such deadly wounds, nor could even the noble Mortimer receive as many wounds as he did and take them all willingly.

Without hesitation, Henry accuses him of lying. Mortimer, he declares, would as soon have encountered the devil himself as Owen Glendower. Henceforth, Percy is not to mention Mortimer's name.

Comment

Glendower's reputed affinity for magic and things diabolical, alluded to here by the King, looks back to the humorous references in the previous scene to Falstaff's compact with the devil.

Hotspur, without delay, is to send his prisoners to the King, or he will hear about it in a form that will not make him happy, Henry asserts. Turning to Northumberland, he says bluntly: "We license your departure with your son. Send us your prisoner, or you will hear of it." The King then leaves with Blunt and his entourage.

To his father, Hotspur insists that he will not send the prisoners if the devil himself should come for them; he is about to follow Henry to tell him so when the elder Percy restrains him. "Are you drunk with choler [anger]?" he asks. At this point, the Earl of Worcester reenters. Hotspur continues to rant, promising to empty his veins and shed his blood drop by drop if he does not raise the "downtrod Mortimer" as high up as the "ingrate and cankered Bolingbroke."

Comment

This last statement comes very close to saying that he will make a king of Mortimer; indeed, one of the unspoken issues between the parties is precisely the nature of the claim which Mortimer can make to the throne. (Of course, Hotspur, we soon learn, has no knowledge of this. It will be brought out into the open shortly.)

Northumberland greets Worcester with the explanation that the King has made young Hotspur mad. Young Percy once more explains that the King wishes to have all his prisoners and adds that the mere mention of a ransom for Mortimer caused the King's face to turn pale, as "on my face he turned an eye of death, trembling even at the name of Mortimer."

Comment

By leaving Hotspur initially in ignorance of the reasons for Henry's fear of Mortimer, Shakespeare can dramatize this most important fact by showing Hotspur's gradual realization of its significance.

Worcester remarks that he does not blame Henry, for had King Richard not proclaimed Mortimer the next in line to the throne? Northumberland agrees, adding that he heard the very proclamation made by Richard prior to his setting forth on his expedition to Ireland (following which he was deposed and murdered).

Comment

Succession to the throne was never a clear issue, and Richard's proclamation by itself would have caused Henry no great concern. But historically, Edmund, Earl of March, by being the grandson of Lionel, Duke of Clarence the second son of Edward III (who died in 1377) had a stronger claim on the throne than Henry Bolingbroke the son of John of Gaunt, himself the third son of Edward III. The Edmund who married the daughter of Owen Glendower, however, was an uncle of Edmund, Earl of March, and was not in the immediate line of succession. Shakespeare has confused the two Edmunds but it is only necessary to know, for the purpose of making sense of the play, that he considers the Edmund who married Owen's daughter to have a strong claim on the throne-a claim which Henry, in the play (later with good reason), imagines Hotspur to be backing with his demands for Mortimer's ransom.

Worcester next laments the fact that their name, rather than Bolingbroke's has been scandalized throughout the world for the murder of Richard. Hotspur (who has apparently discovered for the first time the reason for Henry's fear of Mortimer begins to dwell on the subject. He asks his father if he and Worcester, who "set the crown upon the head of this forgetful man," must suffer the shame of "murtherous subornation" (that is, the reputation of having induced Henry to murder Richard). Will they be cursed as the agents, or worse, the "base second means, the cords, the ladder or the hangman rather?" Then, with a faint suggestion of **irony**, he asks pardon for stooping to such low **themes** to evaluate their position.

Comment

Worcester's concern for public reputation, and Hotspur's mention of crown and hangman, catch up the very same motifs used in the previous scene (here, with a much graver importance). These juxtapositions are the poetic means of suggesting answers to the questions of nobility and honor which are raised in the play.

Hotspur continues his rhetorical questioning and asks if future times will remember them only as men of nobility and power who misused their offices to "put down Richard, that sweet lovely rose, and plant this thorn, this canker, Bolingbroke?" And will you be more shamed than this even, for having been discarded by him when you are no longer of use to him? There is still time to redeem yourselves-to regain honor and reputation in the world. Revenge yourselves upon this proud King, who ponders only the means of your deaths.

Worcester (who, as we soon learn, has been plotting against Henry for some time) tries to calm Hotspur by broaching a "matter deep and dangerous" and "full of peril," but the young man's imagination races far ahead, and he exclaims: "Send danger from the east unto the west, so honor cross it from the north to south, and let them grapple. O, the blood more stirs to rouse a lion than to start a hare." Hotspur then gives vent to a sentiment that has long been regarded by readers of the play as the very key to his character:

"By heaven, methinks it were an easy leap To pluck bright honor from the pale-faced moon, Or dive into the bottom of the deep, Where fathom-line could never touch the ground, And pluck up drowned honor by the locks…"

Comment

Even when we ultimately come to see the limitations of this kind of romantic chivalry - and Hal's understanding of it is a major feature of his growth toward kingship - we never lose sight of its value as well. This is largely the result of the magnificent poetry that Shakespeare writes for Hotspur.

Completely misunderstanding the import of Worcester's words, he ends with a sarcastic cry of "out upon this half-faced fellowship." Worcester continues to try to mollify the hot-tempered youth, and brings up the subject of the Scottish prisoners, whereupon young Percy interrupts once more, exclaiming, "I'll keep them all! By God, he shall not have a Scot of them" Worcester presses on patiently, attempting to explain his plan for the disposal of the prisoners while Hotspur's imagination takes another tack as he imagines himself training a little starling to shout "Mortimer" in the King's ear to keep his ire burning. He solemnly denounces all studies except the ways and means of harassing Bolingbroke. As for the "sword-and-buckler Prince of Wales," he would have him poisoned except that he believes his father has no love for him and would be glad if he met with an accident.

Comment

Hotspur's contemptuous dismissal of the Prince as a roisterer may be partially justified and is in character for Hotspur, in any case, but it later turns out to have been an ironic misreading of character, in view of Hal's subsequent reform and his ultimate vanquishing of Hotspur with "sword and buckler."

Worcester sees that he can get nowhere with Hotspur and makes as if to leave. The elder Percy chastises the youth as an "impatient fool," plying his tongue like a woman, but Hotspur continues. Bolingbroke's presence is like a whip, a scourge, a nettle, the sting of ants. He is a "vile politician," a "king of smiles"; on a former occasion, this "fawning greyhound," proffering a "candy deal of courtesy," used such condescending language to him as "gentle Harry Percy" and "kind cousin." "The devil take such cozeners!" he exclaims.

Comment

There is a pun here, of course, on "cousin" and "cozeners" (pretenders). The language of the Percies is marked by puns to some extent, but the witty sallies of Falstaff and the Prince are markedly superior in the excellence and depth of their ambiguities. While Hotspur's speech may have a more poetic strain, those of Hal and Falstaff have the quality of greater intellectual penetration.

Hotspur's tirade finally at an end, Worcester announces his plan: release all the Scottish prisoners save the son of the Earl of Douglas, who will be a hostage, assuring you of cooperation on the part of the Scots. And you (turning to the elder Percy) shall ingratiate yourself with the Archbishop of York, who "bears hard his brother's death at Bristow."

Comment

The Archbishop of York was Richard Scroop (or Scrope), whose brother William (as Shakespeare believes) are executed at Henry's command in 1399. The rebels can thus count on his support. (William Scroop was actually a member of an allied family-Shakespeare is following an error in his source).

Worcester goes on to say that the plot is fully hatched and awaits only the opportunity of being put into execution. Hotspur is immediately taken with the idea and predicts its success, saying, "I smell it: Upon my life it will do well." To join the power of Scotland and of York with Mortimer cannot fail. But speed is necessary, Worcester maintains. The King already plans our undoing. But he cautions Hotspur to wait until the time is ripe, which will not be long in coming. We will "bear our fortunes in our own strong arms" (with a pun on "arms").

Hotspur closes the scene in a magnificent epitome of his entire attitude so far:

"Uncle, adieu. O, let the hours be short Till fields and blows and groans applaud our sport."

HENRY IV, PART 1

SUMMARY

This scene introduces the third major set of characters, and specifically:

1. It generates the main action (as opposed to **theme**) of the play, That is, the actual rebellion is gotten underway.

2. The disaffection of the King and the Percies is made more understandable and more acute, and the motives for the war are clarified.

3. We get a thorough understanding of the character of Hotspur-at this point, an attractive and courageous young man, even though extremely rash and self-willed.

4. It presents the claim of Mortimer to the throne as the most important issue which divides Henry and the Percies. It is their disenchantment with the form his "gratitude" takes, and his fear that they will urge the claim of Mortimer.

5. This is the third scene - and the third which shows a set of characters plotting to advance their interests. More and more, the audience comes to expect the dramatist's meaning to be presented in the form of analogies rather than direct statements.

6. The instinctive feeling for each other which marks the relationship of the elder and the younger Percy tends to force us to consider the Falstaff-Hal relationship as a spurious father-son pattern, subverting the

natural one which ought to exist between Henry and the Prince. (This is brought out more pointedly in a later scene, in which Falstaff "plays" the King.)

7. Some of the comic by-play on "reputation" and "hangmen," introduced in the previous scene, is here treated in a serious way, underlining yet again the manner in which the comic and the serious **episodes** limit and define each other's meaning.

8. A minor character, Sir Walter Blunt, merely alluded to in Scene 1, is here given a short speech which shows him to be a level-headed individual.

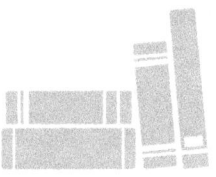

HENRY IV, PART 1

TEXTUAL ANALYSIS

ACT II

ACT II: SCENE 1

The scene is set in an inn-yard in Rochester, where Gadshill has gone to case the prospects for a large haul that night. (We learn in this scene that Gadshill is a "setter" or confederate who lures victims on or sizes them up.) He is in cahoots with the chamberlain (the man who had charge of the bedrooms at the Rochester inn). Two carriers, transporters of goods by horseback, are in the inn-yard at about four in the morning, complaining because their horses are not yet packed for the day's journey. The scene is difficult to understand because of the argot (or slang) that these characters use-slang complicated by more of the sort of riddling and punning observed in <u>Act 1</u>. Furthermore, much of what is said appears to have little connection with the main action and **themes** of the play, though frequently the dramatist uses it to comment ironically or satirically on the poses and actions of characters in the main plot. Of course, the jesting was probably appealing enough for its own sake to the "groundlings" in the contemporary audience for which Shakespeare wrote.

Comment

It has become practically obligatory for every Shakespearean commentator to point out that the Elizabethan audience consisted of a wide cross section of the social community and that a Shakespearean play (like a minstrel show) contained something to appeal to all tastes. The "groundlings" were the members of the lower social groups who paid their penny for the privilege of sitting in the "pit" and responding in frequently raucous fashion to the clowning which they expected as a matter of course.

The first carrier enters and bellows a complaint at the ostler (named Tom) for not packing his horse. He then gives the ostler directions for saddling the horse. A second carrier enters at this point, complaining about the horses' feed and remarks that "this house is turned upside down since Robin Ostler died" calling the inn "the most villainous house in all London for fleas."

Comment

While this is not something the groundlings may be supposed to have caught (nor, indeed, very many of the more literate members of the audience either) the "disordered house" of this conversation mirrors the disorder of the royal house, following the death of Richard II. Puns on "house," taken as "building" and as "family" are of long standing.

HENRY IV, PART 1

The two carriers go on with their complaint about being bitten by fleas and attribute the number of fleas to the "chamber-lye" produced by the necessity of answering nature's calls in the chimney, since chamber pots were scarce. They abuse the ostler again for not hurrying, and the first carrier threatens to break his pate, adding, "Come and be hanged! Hast no faith in thee?"

Comment

A reader who notices that even the offhand threats and jibes here mirror the "hanging" and "faith" motifs introduced in Act I, is coming to understand that the language of a Shakespearean play is not merely an instrument of discourse between characters, but makes up the very fabric or atmosphere of the play, to which even casual utterances must conform, reflecting the major concerns of the drama. The carrier's threat to "break the ostler's pate [skull]" looks ahead to puns in Scene 3 of this act on "broken crowns" (both "coins" and "skulls"), and both of these merge in the major idea of Henry's usurpation of the throne, itself a form of "breaking the crown."

Gadshill now enters and asks one of the carriers for the loan of his lantern; he inquires of them what time they expect to arrive in London. The carriers, apparently seeing skullduggery written all over Gadshill's face, turn him down on both counts. They leave, and the chamberlain enters to inform Gadshill that a franklin (a rich landowner) from Kent, carrying three hundred marks (equal to several thousand dollars today), was up and ready to leave. Gadshill bets his "neck" that they will meet with thieves, but the chamberlain tells him to save it for the hangman. Gadshill says that he will make a "fat pair of gallows" since old Sir John (Falstaff) will hang with him. All puffed up over his familiarity with the Prince, he almost spills the beans about Hal's complicity to the chamberlain by mentioning certain others with him "which for sport sake are content to do the profession some grace," and then, in an amusing catalogue of broken-down thieving types, he adds: "I am joined with no foot land-rakers, no long-staff six-penny strikers, none of these mad mustachio purple-hued maltworms; but with nobility and tranquility …" Gadshill puns on the thieves' habit of "praying to the commonwealth, their saint" (for its "wealth"), and "preying on her" (by making her their "boots" or "spoils"). The chamberlain then matches him in punning by taking "boots" in the sense of "footwear," and asking him if she (the commonwealth) keeps out water. They then jest about the invisibility of thieves (at night) and refer to the popular superstition that fernseed could make a man invisible; finally, with more quibbles about Gadshill's being a "true man" but a "false thief," the scene ends.

Comment

The fernseed superstition looks back to the King's superstitious allusion to "night-tripping fairies," who might have exchanged Hal and Hotspur in their cribs, and ahead to the supernatural dealing of Owen Glendower. The playing on "invisibility" is also a minor anticipation of the battle scene in the last act, when the King in effect becomes "invisible" by having several knights all dress in his armor.

SUMMARY

This puzzling scene thus has four main functions:

1. Its coarse jesting and punning provide entertainment for the groundlings, apart from their organic connection with the main theme.

2. It advances the plot by explaining how Gadshill got wind of the thieves' wealthy victims.

3. It catches up and continues subordinate motifs, such as "truth," "faith," and "hanging."

4. It mirrors the "disordered house" **theme** of the main plot line.

ACT II: SCENE 2

The scene is the highway near Gadshill. The Prince and Poins enter, Poins relating that he has just hidden Falstaff's horse. They retire into the shadows as Falstaff enters, calling for Poins. Hal steps forward, rebuking Sir John for a "fat-kidneyed rascal," and tells him to be quiet. He says that Poins has gone to the top of the hill. Falstaff abuses the "absent" Poins, pretends to be fed up with his antics, and makes a mock threat to kill him, even if he should be hanged for it. He humorously decides that his affection for Poins is the result of a love potion that he has been given: "It could not be else; I have drunk medicines." Crying out on Poins, Hal, Bardolph, and Peto as "stony-hearted villains" for making him walk, he declares "A plague upon it when thieves cannot be true to one another!"

Comment

We see that Falstaff's huge size is something that he too can jest about. Beneath the jesting here, however, there is in the feigned "falling-out" of the thieves, a reflection of the falling out between the King and the Percies.

The Prince again steps forward, calls Sir John a "fat-guts," and tells him to lay his ear to the ground to listen for the sound of travelers on the highway. Falstaff refuses, reflecting that there is no lever at hand to raise him up again. He asks Hal to help him find his horse, and the Prince refuses, exclaiming: "Out, ye rogue! Shall I be your ostler" The fat knight then tells the Prince to go and hang himself in his "own heir-apparent garters" and threatens to turn informer and to have **ballads** composed about the whole lot of them and "sung to filthy tunes." (All of this, of course, with the inimitable flavor of Falstaff's bounding wit.)

Gadshill enters with Bardolph and Peto and cries "Stand!" (a challenge), but Falstaff, unable to take any passing detail with complete seriousness, replies (referring to his size and the absence of his horse): "So I do, against my will." Poins then comes forward, and Gadshill tells them all to don masks, for the victims are approaching. The Prince orders the four to confront the travelers while he and Poins wait below to overtake them if they escape. Peto asks how many of them there are, and Gadshill replies that there are eight or ten. Falstaff wonders aloud who will be robbing whom, and the Prince asks, "What, a coward, Sir John Paunch?" To this, the fat knight (with seeming seriousness) retorts that he is not. The Prince and Poins take their leave.

Comment

While it may never be legitimate to pin labels like that of "coward" on dramatic characters (who are, after all, not flesh-and-blood persons with a fully developed and consistently manifested psychology), the question of cowardice, and its relationship to courage and honor, is obviously a central concern of the play.

The travelers now enter and are challenged by the thieves. Falstaff upbraids them with insulting epithets, calling them "whoreson caterpillars," "bacon-fed knaves," "gorbellied knaves," and "bacons," which, considering the glass house in which Falstaff dwells, are most ungracious terms. They rob and bind them and then retire to a quiet place to divide the spoils. At this point, Poins and the Prince, disguised in buckram suits, set upon Falstaff and the others, who all run away-Falstaff, after striking a blow or two. The Prince laughs at the ease with which they took the booty and, in a famous line, says of Falstaff that he "sweats to death and lards the lean earth as he walks along."

Comment

This is only one of numerous images which depict Falstaff as a repository of oil, fat, grease, tallow, or some other oleaginous substance.

The scene ends with Poins' exclamation, "How the fat rogue roared!"

SUMMARY

This scene contains more action, properly speaking, than any so far. It has the following specific functions:

1. It is the necessary preparation for the later uproarious scene in the Boar's Head Tavern, where the Prince and Poins expose the true facts of the robbery.

2. It adds to the characterization of Sir John Falstaff; in particular, it shows a greater degree of complexity in Falstaff, in such details as his denial that he is a coward, and his obstinate clutch on life, seen in such outcries as "they hate us youth" and "young men must live."

ACT II: SCENE 3

The scene is Warkworth Castle, home of young Hotspur; he enters alone, reading a letter, and making exasperated outbursts concerning the contents. The letter can be reconstructed from his speech, as follows: "But, for mine own part, my lord, I could be well contented to be there, in respect of the love I bear your house ... The purpose you undertake is dangerous, the friends you have named uncertain, the time itself unsorted [poorly chosen], and your whole plot too light for the counterpoise of so great an opposition."

Comment

The author of the letter is not identified, but he is obviously a lord who has been approached by the Percies to support their rebellion against Henry. A reasonable interpretation of his words would make the man out to be merely cautious, but the letter drives Hotspur into an impassioned outburst against his supposed cowardice.

To this man's objection that the plan is dangerous, Hotspur can only reply (in a famous line), "'Tis dangerous to take a cold, to sleep, to drink; but I tell you, my lord fool, out of this nettle, danger, we pluck this flower, safety." He calls him a "cowardly hind," a "frosty-spirited rogue," a "pagan rascal" (for lacking faith in their plan), and a "dish of skim milk." Hotspur's momentary fear that this lord will now inform the King of their plans is quickly dispelled with the thought, "We are prepared. I will set forward to-night."

Comment

Following so closely on the heels of the "cowardly" flight of Falstaff and his cohorts, Hotspur's exclamations about the cowardice of this unnamed lord achieve an extra emphasis. In fact, the parallelism of Hotspur and the Prince - their dramatic pairing-off - is seen to be matched by another parallelism, that between Falstaff and Hotspur. Hotspur, of course, is a much shallower character than Falstaff, and at this early point, before the significance of Falstaff has fully emerged the criterion of judgment between them is "honor," and Hotspur easily carries the day on this score.

Hotspur's wife Kate, enters only to be told by him that he must leave her within two hours. She replies in a rather lengthy speech, ostensibly to ask why she has been in effect banished from his presence lately, but in reality she simply reveals more thoroughly and vividly his monomaniac concern with war and its accoutrements. What, she inquires, has taken from him all stomach (desire), pleasure, and even sleep? Why is he constantly fretful, pale, given to melancholy? Even in sleep, she declares, he mumbles tales of war, guides his steed, and makes outcries to his soldiers.

Comment

The incessancy of Hotspur's preoccupation with war is implied in the catalogue of terms which Kate claims she has heard him recite in sleep:

> "...And thou hast talk'd Of sallies and retires, of trenches, tents, Of palisadoes, frontiers, parapets, Of basilisks, of cannon, culverin, Of prisoners' ransom, and of soldiers slain, And all the currents of a heady fight."

His sweating brow and strange facial expressions have given him, in fact, the appearance of a man whose body and spirit are "at war." These are portents, Kate insists, and she must know what they mean. They are then interrupted by a servant.

Hotspur inquires of the servant if a certain packet of letters has been despatched and if the horses have been brought. One horse has been brought, the servant replies. "That roan shall be my throne," cries young Percy, and then he engages in a witty sally with Kate, who tries playfully to learn his secret, but is finally put off with the comment:

> "...this is no world To play with mammets and to tilt with lips: We must have bloody noses and crack'd crowns, And pass them current too. God's me, my horse!"

Comment

There are important puns here on "current" (money is "currency"), and "crowns" ("crowns" are both coins and heads); the point is that "crack'd crowns" must be made to serve as the currency or money of war. This is Hotspur's normalizing of the abnormal condition of war. Furthermore, a horse is indeed the very emblem of war. Shakespeare's Richard III is remembered for his immortal war-cry, "A horse, a horse, my kingdom for a horse." The parallelism with Falstaff is seen once more in the ludicrous figure he cuts as he looks for his horse, hidden by Poins.

Kate asks her husband for a true answer to the question, "Do you love me?" He replies: "When I am a-horseback, I will swear I love thee infinitely." But he refuses to answer further questions. He trusts her "secrecy" to this extent: she will not utter what she does not know. The scene ends abruptly.

SUMMARY

This short scene introduces Hotspur's wife Kate, and while it cannot be said to develop Hotspur's character any further, it does at least deepen our sense of his total commitment to the martial life. With respect to action and plot it:

1. Shows (in the anonymous lord's refusal) the possibility of the rebellion's backfiring against the Percies.

2. Calls attention to the Falstaff-Hotspur parallelism, through the "horse" and "cowardice" motifs.

3. Establishes that the rebellion is well underway, with Hotspur prepared to leave Warkworth Castle to join the other conspirators (including Mortimer, Scroop, Glendower, and Douglas) by the ninth of the following month.

4. Provides an excellent illustration of Shakespeare's method of "meaning through juxtaposition." The carriers' concern for the packing of their horses, Falstaff's comic search for his horse, and Hotspur's stirring lyrical praise of his mount define one another by contrast. Moreover, Hotspur's identification of "roan" and "throne" relates this set of images to that of thrones, crowns, and kingship.

ACT II: SCENE 4

This is unquestionably one of the great scenes of Shakespearean drama. It takes place in Boar's Head Tavern in Eastcheap, where the Prince and Poins have retreated to wait for Falstaff and the others to return. As the scene opens the Prince joins Ned Poins; he has just been consorting for some time with the menial tavern help, the "drawers," or tapster-waiters. The Prince's tone seems a bit stuffy as he laughs at the condescending airs of the tavern lads who have sought to flatter him with such compliments as these: that though he is but Prince of Wales, he is nevertheless a "king of courtesy"; and that when he is King of England he is sure to have the allegiance of all the "good lads" of Eastcheap. Hal lampoons their customs - that, for example, of requiring anyone who pauses for a breath in his drinking to finish off the flagon in a gulp. He remarks to Poins: "I tell thee, Ned, thou hast lost much honor, that thou were not with me in this action."

Comment

The Prince's attitude is somewhat priggish, to be sure, but at least we can see the beginnings of concern for the true nature of "honor." His supercilious dismissal of the drawers as persons of no consequence may be as shallow in its way, however, as Gadshill's earlier pride over his acquaintance with people of high station who might do his "profession some grace."

Hal has been given a piece of sugar by one of the tapsters (presumably as a gesture of favor). While waiting for Falstaff, and the big joke to be played, he decides to have some fun with the tapster Francis and stations Poins in another room to keep calling for "Francis!" while he detains him, on the pretext of trying to find out why he gave the Prince the sugar. The exchange between Hal and Francis is funny simply for the nonconsecutive absurdity of the dialogue, but it does not lend itself well to summary. The height of nonsense is reached when the Prince asks:

> "Wilt thou rob this leathern-jerkin, crystal-button, not-pated, agate-ring puke-stocking, caddis-garter, smooth-tongue, Spanish-pouch, - [Francis] O Lord, sir, who do you mean? [Prince] Why, then, your brown bastard is your only drink; for look you Francis, your white canvas doublet will sully. In Barbary, sir, it cannot come to so much. [Francis] What, sir?"

Comment

It is tempting to dismiss the entire dialogue as a piece of absurdity, showing the Prince's contemptuous chaffing of the drawer, but there is a serious aspect to it. Hal's remarks to Francis concern the nature of his apprenticeship. At one point the Prince asks him, "Darest thou be so valiant as to play the coward with thy indenture and show it a fair pair of heels and run from it?" In a somewhat remote fashion, Francis' situation mirrors the Prince's, whose own problem can be represented as that of a man "indentured to kingship," and whose actions in "running from it" are related to ideals of "valiancy" and "cowardice." Significantly, this part of the scene ends with Francis standing still in amazement, while the Prince detains him, and Poins summons him loudly.

At this point the vintner-owner enters and rebukes Francis for not answering the calls. He tells the Prince that Falstaff and a half-dozen more are at the door and asks if he should let them in. Hal tells him to let them cool their heels for a while and then to open the door. Poins returns and asks the Prince the point of the jest they have just played on Francis. The Prince makes the enigmatic reply that he is "now of all humors that have showed themselves humors since the old days of goodman Adam to the pupil age of this present twelve o'clock at midnight."

Comment

In Ben Jonson's famous definition of "humors" a person was "humorous" when "someone peculiar quality doth possess [him], that it doth draw all his affects, his spirits, and his powers ... all to run one way." The Prince's reply to Poins may thus be taken either as a simple "I am without motive-I act out of giddiness" or it may be seen as a deeper revelation of the Prince's progress in moral reform. His abandonment to "all humors" may be taken as a symbol of emancipation from the thieves.

Francis reappears, and the Prince marvels that though he is a man, he should have fewer words than a parrot. His "eloquence [is no more than] the parcel of a reckoning." The Prince's mind turns, by way of contrast, to Hotspur, "he that kills me some six or seven dozen of Scots at a breakfast, washes his hands, and says to his wife, "Fie upon this quiet life! I want work."

> **Comment**

We see here that the problem of honor and manhood now takes the form in Hal's mind of the relationship between action and eloquence. In Hotspur, industry, valor, and eloquence are all connected in a way that the Prince does not sympathize with but does not understand completely enough to be able to rise above it. In Francis, there is industry but no eloquence at all. The session with Falstaff (soon to follow) is, among other things, a further analysis of these ideals.

"Call in Falstaff," says the Prince, "I'll play Percy, and that damned brawn shall play Dame Mortimer his wife…. Call in ribs, call in tallow."

> **Comment**

The reference to "playing" parts, suggests the idea that finding one's proper mode of action in life is in some ways analogous to acting a role. This is also related to the **theme** of "appearance and reality." Shakespeare develops these **themes** more explicitly in later plays, such as Hamlet and Lear, but they are present here as well. Hal must learn to "see through" the specious ways of ordering life represented by both Falstaff and young Percy.

Here Falstaff, Gadshill, Bardolph, and Peto enter-Falstaff swaggering in superiority over the "cowards," Poins and Hal, who have "abandoned" them during the robbery. "A plague of all cowards!" cries Falstaff, "give me a cup of sack, rogue. Is there no virtue extant?" He then complains that there is lime in the sack, another example of the roguery of "villainous man." Yet a coward is worse than that. "There lives not three good men unhanged in England; and one of them is fat and grows old." The Prince eggs him on, and Falstaff scornfully rejects him as "a king's son!" adding, "If I do not beat thee out of thy kingdom with a dagger of lath ... I'll never wear hair on my face more. You Prince of Wales!" Sir John then calls the Prince a coward, and Hal threatens to stab him, whereupon Falstaff retreats to the safer ground of sarcasm. He says that he will be damned before he calls the Prince "coward," but adds that he would give a thousand pounds to be able to run as fast as he can. "A plague upon such backing! Give me them that will face me. Give me a cup of sack. I am a rogue if I drunk today." At the Prince's insistence, Falstaff explains the reason for his bad temper. They had taken a thousand pounds that morning, and it had been stolen from them through Hal's and Poins' failure to show up at the appointed place.

A hundred men set upon the four of them, Falstaff lies, and they fought for two solid hours. His doublet was pierced eight times, his hose four, his shield "hacked like a handsaw." Gadshill notes that the four of them attacked a dozen men, and Falstaff corrects him - there were sixteen, at least, and when they had finished the sixteen had been bound tight. As they were sharing the loot, another band set upon them (but only after freeing the first sixteen). "What, fought you with them all?" asks the Prince. To which Sir John replies: "All? I know not what you call all, but if I fought not with fifty of them, I am a bunch of radish. If there were not two or three and fifty upon poor old Jack, then am I no two-legg'd creature." To this Hal ironically retorts that he hopes Sir John has not murdered some of them. But the fat knight says it is too late for hopes of that sort, he has certainly killed two of them-two rogues in buckram suits.

Comment

The humor of Falstaff's exaggerations hardly comes through in bare summary. But the number grows, with each detail added, to four, then seven, nine, and finally, eleven.

The Prince exclaims, "O monstrous! eleven men grown out of two!" Whereupon Falstaff includes an additional "three misbegotten knaves in Kendal green," who came up behind and attacked him in the dark. Hal's vituperation now knows no bounds, and he bursts out: "These lies are like their father that begets them; gross as a mountain, open, palpable. Why thou clay-brained guts, thou knotty-pated fool, thou whoreson, obscene, greasy tallow-catch, - "And he demands of the fat knight a reason for his lies. Falstaff refuses to give a reason "on compulsion," and the Prince attacks him with more outrageous epithets, receiving a string of them from Falstaff in return (including, "you dried neat's-tongue, you bull's pizzle, you stockfish ... you sheath, you bowcase" - all images of leanness).

Finally, the Prince tells all; how they saw the four of them set on four travelers and rob them; how the two of them then "outfaced them from their prize"; how Falstaff "carried his guts away nimbly ... and roared for mercy." Hal ends by asking Sir John what dodge he can use now to hide from the shame of this open revelation. And Poins taunts him also: "Come, let's hear, Jack; what trick hast thou now?" Falstaff's reply is one of the most memorable of Shakespearean speeches: "By the Lord, I knew ye as well as he that made ye." And he pretends that out of instinct he was simply unable to turn upon the Prince. He was a coward upon instinct. But he is glad they have the money. Let the doors be locked, and a play be performed extempore. The Prince suggests that the argument (or plot) ought to be Sir John's running away.

Comment

Hal thus shows that his sense of proportion, at this moment at least, is not as good as Falstaff's.

"Ah," replies Falstaff, "no more of that, Hal, and thou lovest me!" The hostess enters to tell the Prince that there is a courtier (she calls him "a nobleman of the court") come from his father to speak with him. The Prince jests about him contemptuously, and Falstaff makes a joke about "gravity" being out of his bed at midnight (the courtier is an elderly man), and goes to send him packing. While Sir John is out of the room, the Prince finds out from the others that Falstaff had hacked his sword with his dagger and had made them tickle their noses with speargrass to make them bleed and promise to swear it was the blood of true men.

Comment

The many casual references to "true men" in the subplot are one of the ways in which it mirrors the major **theme** of "honor."

Falstaff returns, and the Prince wishes to resume the badinage, chiding Falstaff about the number of years that have passed since he was able to see his own knee. But Sir John informs him that the knight who had appeared at the door was Sir John Bracy, who had come to report to the Prince that he must return to court, for young Percy, Glendower, Mortimer, the elder Percy, and Douglas ("that runs a-horseback up a hill perpendicular") have committed themselves to rebellion. And he adds: "thy father's beard is turned white with the news: you may buy land now as cheap as stinking mackerel." The Prince replies in an offhand fashion that in that case, if it should be a hot June they will be able to buy maidenheads by the hundreds.

HENRY IV, PART 1

But Falstaff is in haste to change the subject back to the dangers of war, and the threat posed to Hal by three such enemies as Hotspur, Douglas, and Glendower. "Art thou not horribly afraid? Doth not thy blood thrill at it?" he asks. The Prince denies that it does.

Comment

There is an odd reversal of roles here, as Falstaff begins to consider seriously the effects of war, and the Prince only reaffirms his devil-may-care attitude. This is perhaps Shakespeare's way of underlining the fact that Hal has reached the ultimate point of disaffection from his father's concerns.

The thought of appearing before his royal father seems now to have a sobering effect upon Hal, and he accepts Falstaff's offer to stand for King Henry in a mock interrogation scene so that he may practice his answers. Falstaff calls for a cup of sack "to make his eyes red" so that he may be thought to have been weeping. He must speak in passion, imitating King Cambyses.

Comment

This is a reference to a character named Cambyses in an earlier play (not by Shakespeare). He has become almost a symbol of empty rhetorical ranting. This may be a slur upon the King's actual or imagined insincerity, or possibly simply upon the shallow tastes of the court caste), or it may be simply another sample of Falstaff's self-conscious exaggeration.

The Prince bows, and Falstaff begins, while the tavern hostess sheds tears of laughter. Falstaff includes her in the mock-pageant, saying, in the mechanical prettiness of so much earlier iambic **pentameter** stage poetry:

> "Weep not, sweet queen; for trickling tears are vain ... For God's sake, lords, convey my tristful queen; For tears do stop the flood-gates of her eyes."

Comment

The ineptness of this verse may be seen in four things:

1. the strictly end-stopped lines

2. the forced **alliteration** ("trickling tears")

3. the absurd coinage ("tristful" queen), and

4. the hackneyed and exaggerated **metaphor** ("floodgates of her eyes")

This is what Falstaff means by "Cambyses' vein," and it may be no more than a topical reference to the work of Shakespeare's less imaginative contemporaries, writing for the stage. But it may also glance at the "niceness" of court society, as seen from the point of view of Falstaff himself.

Falstaff (as King Henry) now addresses himself to the Prince. He marvels at the way in which Hal spends his time. And he uses an image drawn from natural history to enforce the idea of wasting youth through bad company. "For though the camomile, the more it is trodden on, the faster it grows, so youth, the more it is wasted the sooner it wears."

> Comment

As it has long been observed, this is an obvious **parody** of the "euphuistic" style (that is, of the style-precious and affected- made famous from its employment in the work of John Lyly entitled Euphues, His England. As in the case of the "Cambyses" style, it also lampoons the affectations of court life.

Much of the humor of the **parody** comes from Falstaff's mixing it with broadly comic statements, such as, "That thou art my son, I have partly thy mother's word, partly my own opinion but chiefly a villainous trick of thine eye and a foolish hanging of thy nether lip that doth warrant me." He then goes on with another euphuistic comparison - this time of Hal's companions with the substance known as pitch. As pitch defiles, so does bad company. "And yet," he goes on, "there is a virtuous man whom I have often noted in thy company, but I know not his name." He is a "portly man," with a "cheerful look, a pleasing eye, and a most noble carriage ... his name is Falstaff.... Harry, I see virtue in his looks.... Him keep with, the rest banish."

> Comment

Beneath the obvious humor, this playing of the father role by Falstaff points to the serious perversion of social and family order which Hal's (perhaps unconscious) adoption of Falstaff as "father-image" has brought about.

In another contest of wit they now exchange places, Falstaff playing the Prince, and Hal playing his father. Of course, the Prince-King's evaluation of Falstaff is quite different. He is a "devil ... in the likeness of an old fat man," a "roasted Manningtree ox with the pudding in his belly," and so forth. With feigned surprise, Falstaff (as Prince) asks, "Whom means your grace?" He replies: "That villainous abominable misleader of youth, Falstaff, that old white-bearded Satan."

Comment

The Prince, in his speech, tries to outdo Falstaff in humorous parodies of affectation. But he is clearly no match for the fat knight.

Falstaff (still playing the Prince) defends himself in a magnificent argument. To be old is not to be taken as an indictment but as a cause for pity; and he admits to being old. But as for being a lecher, that he denies. Is sack and sugar a fault? Is to be old and merry a sin? If the fat man is to be hated, then Pharaoh's lean kine are to be loved. "Banish not him thy Harry's company. Banish plump Jack, and banish all the world."

Comment

Falstaff's defense is more than a mere bit of trumpery. Cutting below the level of clever retort is the audience's instinctive and healthy response to the good aspects of appetite and its fulfillment. Falstaff is, whatever else he may be, an impressive symbol of human nature's resistance to puritanical repression.

Bardolph enters on the run, to announce that the sheriff is at the door. He is followed by the hostess with the same news, who wishes to know whether she should let them in. The Prince directs Falstaff and the others to hide behind the arras (wall tapestry) while he and Peto remain to greet the sheriff. The sheriff announces that he is looking for a "gross fat man" in connection with the robbery of three hundred marks. Hal, lying, denies that he is there, but promises to send him to the sheriff on the morrow. After the sheriff departs, Peto discovers Falstaff fast asleep behind the arras.

Comment

This detail has been enlisted in support of the theory that Falstaff is no coward, on the principle that a coward could not so calmly have gone off to sleep while the inn was being searched. It is interesting to note that once this kind of psychological interpretation of character is admitted as possible at all, all sorts of alternative explanations present themselves. Perhaps it was from sheer exhaustion-or an excess of sack. No plausible explanation can be denied.

The Prince goes through Falstaff's pockets and finds a paper containing a list of expenditures - a total of 10s. 6d. (ten shillings and sixpence) for sack, capons, and anchovies, but only a halfpenny for bread. The Prince calls it monstrous - this intolerable deal of sack. But his mood changes as he announces to Peto that they will be off to the wars on the next day, and that he intends to procure the captaincy of a troop of foot soldiers for Sir John. The money (that stolen from the travelers) will be paid back with interest. The scene finally closes with Peto's "Good morrow, my lord."

Comment

This serious intention to go to the wars, and the Prince's concern for the repayment of the stolen money, show that he is about to "throw off the unyoked humor of their idleness," which he had promised in his opening soliloquy. It is a good omen for the future course of the war, and a fitting close for this second act.

SUMMARY

This scene is limitlessly rich in action of its own, in **parody** of the main action of the play, and in symbolic detail. A few of its chief accomplishments are:

1. The Prince's character undergoes a radical change, objectified in his reactions to the "drawers," his riddling interrogation of Francis, and his two King-Prince dialogues with Falstaff. His serious demeanor at the close of the scene is the very natural result of the Prince's psychological introspection, of which this scene is a symbolic embodiment.

2. It contains comic reflections of a number of serious features of the main plot: Specifically:

    a. The Prince's evaluation of Francis shows analogies to his own situation-his "bondage to the claims of kingship."

    b. The mock King-Prince dialogues anticipate the serious conference between Hal and his father which will take place in the next act.

    c. The "encounter" on the highway is a comic anticipation of the later battle of Shrewsbury. Even the disguises of Hal and Poins find a parallel in Henry's king-surrogates, wearing his armor to deceive the enemy.

3. The characterization of Falstaff is deepened. We see him as robber, fugitive, liar, mock-king, mock-prince, prince's representative (to Bracy at the door), and finally (only by Hal's mention of it), as a captain of foot soldiers. His symbolic scope and universal appeal are made more concretely realizable.

4. We meet a number of rather undifferentiated minor characters: Bardolph, Peto, Francis, the vintner, the hostess, and the sheriff. They at least provide a sense of Hal's motion through a well-defined social milieu, as well as contributing to the action of the scene.

5. The motifs of "hanging," "ruth," and, especially, "cowardice," as well as others, receive their imaginative orchestration once more.

6. There are, finally, a number of independently funny details:

    a. Hal's joke at Francis' expense

    b. the riotous exaggerations of Falstaff, and his magnificent evasions

    c. the parodies of the stylistic affectations of "high society," such as "euphuism"

    d. Falstaff's falling asleep, and the humorous inventory found in his pocket.

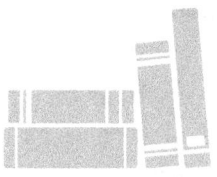

HENRY IV, PART 1

TEXTUAL ANALYSIS

ACT III

ACT III: SCENE 1

The scene is Owen Glendower's castle in Wales. Hotspur, Worcester, Mortimer, and Glendower enter, speaking of the prospects for success in their revolt against the crown. Mortimer is optimistic and calm. Hotspur is in his customary choleric humor. They are consulting a map of England, on which they are attempting to trace out an equitable division of the country among Glendower, Mortimer, and young Percy. Glendower invites them all to sit, and calling Hotspur by name, remarks: "For by that name as oft as Lancaster doth speak of you, his cheek looks pale and with a rising sigh he wisheth you in heaven."

Comment

Glendower may mean not only that the very thought of young Percy drives Henry mad, but that the martial **connotations** of the name "Hotspur" act as a focus for his rage at their rebellion. The audience, of course, also realizes that the King's anger is partially bred of his resentment of Hal's failure to measure up to Hotspur.

Hotspur returns the compliment by telling Glendower that Henry wishes him in hell whenever he hears his name. This is the signal for Glendower to embark upon a fantastic recital of the marvelous occurrences which attended his nativity. The brow of heaven was "full of fiery shapes of burning cressets," and the "frame and huge foundation of the earth shaked like a coward."

Comment

We are suddenly introduced to the strange personality of Glendower, which Shakespeare derived partly from the chronicles, but probably also filled out with other suggestions of occult interests, based on the notion that his audience would be entertained by having their concept of the Welsh as "provincials" amply illustrated on the stage.

Hotspur pooh-poohs Glendower's claim and ridicules him, but the Welshman insists that his story is true, whereupon young Percy, in an amusing metaphor, interprets the shaking of the earth not as the result of awe and fear, but simply as a strange eruption of old mother Earth, who was "with a kind of colic pinched and vexed by the imprisoning of unruly wind within her womb." Glendower, still holding to his patience, tells Hotspur that he does not take this sort of rebuke from many men, and once more calmly reiterates his fantastic account, adding that "all the courses of my life do show I am not in the roll of common men." And he asks where the man is who has ever been able to teach him anything. Where is that

"... woman's son Can trace me in the tedious ways of art
And hold me pace in deep experiments?"

Comment

The word "experiments" still had in Shakespeare's day the suggestion of illicit, occult tampering with nature. In presenting Glendower as a lusus naturae (or "sport of nature"), Shakespeare may be underlining his **theme** of the connection between the harmony of nature and the order of society. Glendower is to "natural" men what Falstaff and the other thieves are to "orderly" men - an enormity.

Hotspur once more shows his contempt, and Mortimer warns him not to tempt Glendower's rage; Hotspur ignores this advice, and when Glendower goes on to tell him that he has the power to command the devil to appear, Hotspur replies that in that event he himself would have the power to shame him away, and he taunts Glendower three times with the jibe, "Tell truth and shame the devil!" Mortimer tries to terminate the dispute, but Glendower replies:

"Three times hath Henry Bolingbroke made head Against my power; thrice from the banks of Wye And sandy-bottom'd Severn have I sent him Bootless home and weather-beaten back."

Comment

Glendower's almost mystical emphasis on the "three-fold aspect of his encounter with Henry, sets off the impatience of Hotspur's triple repetition of the insult about shaming the devil, and the very practical "tripartite" division of the kingdom which is about to take place. This is one very minor way of underlining the necessity for coming out from behind the screen of language when expediency demands it.

With another quibble (identical with that of Gadshill and the Chamberlain) about "boots" and "foul weather," they begin the serious business of settling the division of the spoils. The archdeacon has arranged three portions. All of England south and east of the Trent and Severn rivers is to go to Mortimer; all of Wales west of the Severn is to be Glendower's; and to young Percy has been assigned all the remainder northward from the Trent. Mortimer, who apparently regards this as a very equitable arrangement, says that they can sign the agreement this very night, and he changes the subject to their eventual meeting at Shrewsbury field with Worcester and Northumberland. "My father Glendower," he says, is not yet ready, but will not be required for a full two weeks. Glendower promises to arrive in a shorter space of time and bids them take their leave of their wives, "For there will be a world of water shed upon the parting of your wives and you."

Comment

Glendower, of course, is not Mortimer's father but his father-in-law, but the reference here alerts us to another father-son relationship like the King-Prince and Falstaff-Hal relationships; these all mirror in their various ways some underlying ideal father-son pattern, which Shakespeare's method does not permit him to deal with explicitly.

But all is not to go as smoothly as Mortimer and Glendower would like it; Hotspur has some thoughts of his own about a proper division of the land. The curve of the River Trent, he complains, "cuts me from the best of all my land / A huge half-moon, a monstrous cantle out." He threatens to have it dammed up so that it will not wind so deeply and rob him of so rich a piece of land.

Comment

This is one of the most important examples of the way in which the very same qualities of spirit that make Hotspur's "nobility" possible can cause this nobility to degenerate into selfish obstinacy and quibbling over trifles.

Mortimer defends the division, pointing out that his portion suffers the same sort of bend in the river, and Worcester intervenes to make a slight modification agreeable to both Mortimer and Hotspur. This time Glendower demurs, saying, "I will not have it altered." He and young Percy almost come to blows, particularly since Hotspur taunts him again for speaking with a Welsh accent. With considerable restraint, the Welshman explains that he learned to speak English as a child at the English court where, even at a young age, he had "framed to the harp / Many an English ditty lovely well, / And gave the tongue a helpful ornament." To Hotspur, this makes him nothing more than a "ballad-monger." Nothing sets his teeth so on edge as "mincing poetry." Glendower yields and agrees to have the line altered, but Hotspur cannot accept this with good grace, and he rubs it in, saying that while he would give thrice so much land to a well-deserving friend, "in the way of bargain, mark ye me, / I'll cavil on the ninth part of a hair." After remarking on the manner in which his daughter dotes on her husband Mortimer, Glendower makes his exit.

Mortimer chides Hotspur for crossing Glendower, but Hotspur asserts that he cannot help himself since the Welshman angers him so by telling him

> "Of the dreamer Merlin and his prophecies, And of a dragon and a finless fish, A clip-wing'd griffin and a moulten raven, A couching lion and a ramping cat, And such a deal of skimble-skamble stuff As puts me from my faith."

Comment

From one point of view this is all "skimble-skamble stuff' (nonsense), but it shows Hotspur's complete refusal to believe in occult predictions (not unlike Macbeth's failure to understand the prophecies of the weird Sisters). The couching lion and the ramping cat suggest the couchant and rampant animals of heraldry and make it appear that there might be a lesson or a warning that Hotspur could profit from if he could muster enough sympathy for the point of view represented by Glendower. The **imagery** of lions is especially important-Falstaff has told Halt hat he is as "valiant as a lion," and now Mortimer will shortly say of Glendower that he is "valiant as a lion." And in Scene 3 of this same act Falstaff will compare King Henry to a lion.

Mortimer tries to convince young Percy that Glendower holds himself in check only because he has a high respect for him. He warns Hotspur not to try it too often. Worcester concurs, and admonishes his nephew to "amend his fault." Sometimes, he says, it shows "greatness, courage, blood." Yet at other times it presents "harsh rage, defect of manners, want of government, pride, haughtiness, opinion, and disdain." The least of these things can bring a nobleman into disrepute.

> Comment

Hotspur shrugs this off, and his contempt for "good manners" illuminates once more the problem of conduct which besets the young Prince. The difference is that Hal is introspective, while Hotspur is completely the extrovert.

Glendower reenters at this point with his daughter and Kate. Mortimer bemoans the fact that he can speak no Welsh and his wife no English. She is weeping over his departure.

> Comment

The motif of "speech as a barrier to understanding," which has been treated so far only abstractly and by implication, here receives a form of concrete symbolism in the husband and wife who are separated by a wall of language.

Glendower speaks to her in Welsh, and from his explanation that "she is desperate here. A peevish self-willed harlotry. / One that no persuasion can do good upon," we see still another repetition of the parent-recalcitrant child figure (King-Prince, Northumberland-Hotspur). She speaks in Welsh, and Mortimer makes a very touching speech, explaining that though they are separated by differing tongues they have a mutual understanding of the language of love. But he finally shows his frustration at their inability to communicate, and Glendower translates for him. She is asking him to lie down and rest his head upon her lap, so that she may on his eyelids "crown the god of sleep," and "making such difference 'twixt wake and sleep / As is the difference betwixt day and night."

Comment

This is yet another version of the "crown" motif, and the day-night inversion of the band of thieves.

Hotspur mimics what he considers to be the foolish antics of Mortimer and his wife by saying to Kate: "Come Kate, thou art perfect in lying down; come, quick, quick, that I may lay my head in thy lap." She jibes at him in return, telling him that he is "altogether governed by humors" (we recall that Hal has described himself as being "of all humors"). The lady sings in Welsh, and Hotspur asks Kate to sing also. When she refuses (with a very mild oath), he tells her she swears like a "comfit-maker's wife," and implores her to swear "mouth-filling" oaths, and leave the "pepper-gingerbread / To velvet-guards and Sunday citizens." She still refuses to sing. All leave the stage.

SUMMARY

There is an astonishingly small amount of genuine action in this scene; in fact, there is hardly any advance, properly speaking, even through the conversations which take place. But it fills out the imaginative texture of the play, and accomplishes these specific things:

1. Action completed: (a) Mortimer, Hotspur, and Glendower (prematurely, as it happens) anticipate their ultimate victory by dividing the country among them; (b) Hotspur and Mortimer agree to meet Glendower at Shrewsbury fourteen days hence, but Glendower agrees to make it in a shorter time.

2. There is presented another side altogether of Hotspur's character. We see that nobility can

degenerate into braggadocio; soldierly firmness into sheer obstinacy; and manly argument into petulant carping.

3. The "father-son" (more broadly the "parent-child") relationship is shown in new guises, altering us once more to the complexity of Hal's situation as a recalcitrant son. Specific instances are:

4. Mortimer's willing compliance with his "father Glendower's" demands.

5. The "peevish self-willed harlotry" of Glendower's daughter.

6. Several verbal motifs come in for repetition in new contexts. Some of these are:

7. Valiancy-Mortimer calls Glendower "valiant as a lion."

8. Crowns-Mortimer's wife will "crown the god of sleep" on his eyelids.

9. Humors-Hotspur is now altogether "governed by humors."

10. "Devilishness" - Hotspur's opinion of Glendower's diabolical interests mirrors, for one thing, Poins' jesting reference to Falstaff's pact with the Devil.

11. The necessity of understanding the distance which separates speech from inner character and intention reappears in Glendower's brand of verbal affectation;

in fact, the important idea of language as a barrier to action achieves concrete representation in Mortimer's relationship with his wife, since neither of them can understand the other's language.

12. The **theme** of "order" is brought into connection with that of "nature," and it achieves some symbolic concreteness in the "harmony of song" which appears in this scene.

ACT III: SCENE 2

The scene is London once again - the palace. The King, the Prince of Wales, and several lords enter. The King asks them to leave him alone for a time with Harry, but to remain close by since he will soon have need of them. They go out and Henry immediately begins upon a tongue-lashing of the Prince. Is God punishing him, he wonders, for some sin of his past life? Is God, in His "secret doom," breeding revenge and a scourge for him?

Comment

"Doom" originally meant merely judgment, but it began to take on the **connotation** of "evil judgment," until finally it came to mean something like "terrible fate." It seems to carry suggestions of both meanings here.

Henry states with some sarcasm that he believes Hal has been appointed by Heaven as an instrument of his punishment. How else, he inquires, "Could such inordinate and low desires, / Such poor, such bare, such lewd, such mean attempts, / Such barren pleasures, rude society," as the Prince is now "grafted to," hold a place in his princely heart?

Comment

Words such as "inordinate" and "grafted" bring in once again the themes of order and nature. "Inordinate" means excessive, but it carries the **connotation** of "failure to observe order." Similarly, the Prince, as Henry sees it, is not merely going through a passing phase of wayward behavior but is involved in a kind of unnatural "symbiosis" with Falstaff and the others. (Stated thus baldly, these ideas seem to be given an exaggerated importance. They really act as subdued metaphors, fleshing out a major pattern of imagery in the play.)

Hal submissively admits to guilt in some of the things he has been charged with, but alleges that he could doubtless clear himself of many others. In any event, he asks his royal father to excuse these things as the faulty wanderings and irregularity of his youth, and to pardon him for his true submission. "God pardon thee!" rejoins Henry.

Comment

This emphasizes again the magnitude of Hal's dereliction from obedience. His offense is against the ideal of sovereignty, and consequently much graver than ordinary filial disobedience.

The King goes on with his angry spate of words, accusing the Prince of failing to meet the traditions of his ancestors, of allowing his place in council to be taken over by his younger brother, and of being an alien to the hearts of all the

King's courtiers. His youthful promise has been dashed, and everyone is predicting his eventual failure. Henry now harks back to the days of his own youth. If he had been so lavish with his company, such a common spectacle, "opinion, that did help [him] to the crown," would have remained with Richard and left him in banishment.

Comment

This is a reference to events covered in Shakespeare's Richard II, in which the exiled Bolingbroke, through strength of character and arms, and with the support of loyal followers, was able to return and overthrow the King. There is, perhaps, some **irony** in the fact that an important element in the "opinion" that helped him to the crown (namely, the Percies), is now trying to help him away from it.

As the King goes on, the serious purpose of his speech begins to take on the coloration of vanity as he speaks of having been wondered at like a comet and of men pointing him out to their children. He evaluates his accomplishments in those days in a speech which in some ways resembles (even while it contrasts markedly with) Hotspur's words about "plucking bright honor from the pale-faced moon":

> "And then I stole all courtesy from heaven, And dress'd myself in such humility That I did pluck allegiance from men's hearts, Loud shouts and salutations from their mouths, Even in the presence of the crowned King."

Only thus, says Henry, did he keep his person unsullied. His presence was like a "robe pontifical" (a pope's ceremonial garment), and his person was seen so rarely that it "showed like a feast" and won "solemnity." Richard II, a skipping king [who] ambled up and down / With shallow jesters," only succeeded in having his name profaned and scorned. He mingled with the hoi-polloi, and became a common sight on the streets of London; he "enfeoffed himself to popularity," and thus like honey, when it is eaten in excess, became an object of loathing rather than love. He began to resemble the cuckoo in men's eyes-heard but not regarded. He was seen only by sick and blunted eyes, such as "afford no extraordinary gaze / Such as is bent on sun-like majesty / When it shines seldom in admiring eyes." In short, the people were "glutted, gorged, and full" with his presence, and that is exactly what the Prince is going to face. He has lost his "princely privilege with vile participation." Every eye is weary of him, complains Henry, save his own, which is now blinding itself with foolish tenderness (he is weeping).

Comment

There are a number of important aspects to this speech: (l) It can hardly be said to advance the action or to bring about the Prince's reform; this is something we know he has already decided upon, and Henry's words on this subject closely echo Hal's earlier soliloquy. (2) It does give greater insight into Henry's character, showing the strength of purpose and the strength of personality which have been his strongest assets, but also revealing a certain vanity in his nature. The "courtesy" which he says he stole from Heaven may be the same "candy deal of courtesy" which Hotspur despises him for, and the same courtesy (seen as "courtly manners") which Falstaff lampoons in the mock interview with the Prince. (3) His reference to the kingly presence as a "sun-like majesty" catches up the earlier night-day symbolism and gives us a new way of looking at Hal's reform-as an entrance into the sunlight of the moral capability of kingship. This symbol will reappear in later scenes.

The Prince at this point promises his royal father that he will hereafter "be more myself," and we may take this as the turning point of the play from the standpoint of Hal's progress in reform. But Henry persists in excoriating his son. Even Hotspur has more right to succeed to the throne, he says, for he fills battlefields, rushes into the jaws of the lion, and leads even lords and bishops into bloody battles. He has won undying honor in his conquest of Douglas. Hotspur, a "Mars in swaddling clothes" and an "infant warrior," took the measure of the great Douglas and made a friend of him, "To fill the mouth of deep defiance up / And shake the peace and safety of our throne." But why does he speak of these enemies, the King goes on, when his own son is his nearest and dearest enemy. He is likely, through fear, base inclination, or spleen, to enter Percy's service and fight against the crown. This is the **climax** and crowning insult of Henry's tirade, and we learn much about the Prince's true character from his calm reply and his impassioned promise to best Motspur if they should meet in battle.

"When I will wear a garment all of blood And stain my favors [features] in a bloody mask, Which, wash'd away, shall scour my shame with it;"

Comment

This is at once a realistic vision of the perils of war, and a poignant expression of the Prince's sense of the true extent of his need for redemption. For he is speaking, in effect, of a "baptism of blood," which will ready him for entrance upon a "new life" of kingship.

All the honors which are now Percy's asserts the Prince, will then be his. He will call Percy to strict account, and make him "render every glory up," and he swears a solemn oath before his father to die a hundred thousand deaths before he should break the smallest part of this promise. The King is finally convinced of Harry's sincerity, and he applauds his speech with a ringing cry: "A hundred thousand rebels die in this. / Thou shalt have charge and sovereign trust herein." This means, of course, that Hal will be given command of an army. At this juncture, Sir Walter Blunt enters with the news that the Scot Douglas and the English rebels had joined forces at Shrewsbury field on the eleventh of the month and that this betokens foul play for the land. The King replies that the "news" is five days old, that Westmoreland and Lord John (Hal's younger brother) have already been dispatched to the battlefield, and that on the following Wednesday, Prince Hal and the King himself will set out with separate forces to meet twelve days hence at Bridgenorth. He closes the scene with a rhyming **couplet**: "Our hands are full of business. Let's away; / Advantage feeds him fat while men delay."

SUMMARY

This scene consists largely of reflective discourse rather than action, but it has a number of subtle functions:

1. Taking Hal's reform as the central "action" of the play, we find here the most important dramatization of his inner struggle and his decision for good over evil. The speeches of the King and Prince are in a sense ceremonial evaluations of actions which have been presented concretely in the first two acts.

2. While Hotspur may have been given the best flights of poetic fancy, Henry's speeches, in their length,

poise, regularity, and formality, reflect something of the dignified nature of regal sway. This is also true of Hal's speeches (though not to the same extent), and it allows the scene to be read as a version of the "contest of wits," farcical and ironic examples of which have already been presented in the earlier Prince-Falstaff exchanges and in the comic by-play among some of the minor characters.

3. Several major images and leading ideas come in for further qualification. For example:

   a. The failure of "order" is seen here, for one thing, as "inordinate desire."

   b. "Honor" appears to the King in his speech as "opinion" and courtesy."

   c. We meet again in new contexts the images of crown, sun, and lion.

   d. The "speech versus action" figure appears in Henry's **metaphor** for Hotspur, who "filled the mouth of deep defiance up" in conquering and making an ally of Douglas.

   e. The image of "masking" (looking back to the vizards worn by the thieves during the robbery at Gadshill, and ahead to the knights disguised in the King's livery) can be seen in the Prince's promise to "stain his favors in a bloody mask" on the field at Shrewsbury.

4. From the standpoint of the war of rebellion as the main "action" of the play, the action is advanced by having Hal given command of an army, and by the King's decision to join forces in Bridgenorth twelve days hence. We also learn (the King reports it to Sir Walter Blunt) that Prince John and Westmoreland have already set out for Shrewsbury with their forces.

5. This scene is a good illustration of the fact that the noble figures do not speak in quibbles and puns, though there is ample opportunity to pick up certain terms for their ambiguities. It would be unthinkable, for instance, for Henry when he mentions his "sceptre and his soul to boot" (or for Hal) to pun on the alternative meanings of "boot" as Falstaff might do, or as both Gadshill and Hotspur have done. It is one way of defining kingly poise and presence as a kind of superiority to quibbling. What is lost through an inability to examine the subtle implications of language is more than made up for in an increased power to make swift unequivocal evaluations and to come to practical decisions.

ACT III: SCENE 3

We are once again in the Boar's Head Tavern in Eastcheap. Falstaff and Bardolph enter chaffing one another, Falstaff, as usual, getting the better of it. He is undergoing another bout of mock repentance. His skin is hanging slack about his bones, he says, his strength is lessening, and the need for repentance is upon him. He has practically forgotten what the inside of a church looks like, he adds, and it is nothing but "company, villainous company," that has been his ruination.

Comment

Falstaff's absurd pretense of reform mirrors the Prince's genuine concern for the remolding of his own life; it is appropriate here, considering that we have just witnessed Hal's earnest protestations of the great change which he is going to bring about in his life.

When Bardolph tells Sir John that his fretfulness will bring him an early death, Falstaff calls for a bawdy song to make him merry. His life was indeed once virtuous enough, he maintains; he swore only a little, played at dice no more than seven times a week, visited a bawdy house no oftener than four times an hour, and lived well and in "good compass." Now he lives out of all order, out of all compass. To which Bardolph replies that he is out of all compass because he is so fat.

Comment

Here we see another - this time a ludicrous - version of "order," the ordered existence of a man whose concept of "gentleman" and of "virtue" shows that he inhabits an ethical and moral vacuum. Bardolph puns on the word "compass" (meaning both "control" and "rotundity"), and this underscores the connection between the irregularity of Falstaff's life and his tremendous girth.

Sir John retorts by abusing Bardolph for his face. It shines so (he is an inveterate toper) that it is like the fleet flagship with its signal lantern (his nose). Still in his "repentance" vein, Falstaff remarks that he can nevertheless make good use of it. As another man might use a death's head or a memento mori (reminders of man's final worldly end), he will use Bardolph's face to remind him of hellfire and the suffering Dives (Luke 16:19-31). It is a fiery angel that he might swear by, an ignis fatuus or a ball of wildfire, a bonfire which has saved Sir John a thousand marks (which he has not had to spend for torches to light his way at night).

Comment

In one way this is a humorous parallel to the ideal of "sun-like majesty" which Henry has held up to the Prince in the previous scene.

The hostess enters, only to be insulted in her turn by being called "Dame Partlet the hen," a reference to Chaucer's Pertelote (hence, a garrulous woman). Falstaff wants to know if she has yet discovered who picked his pocket, and she replies that the house has been turned upside-down and not a trace has been found. He insults her further by suggesting that she is a loose woman and that the inn is a place for lewd carryings-on. Accusations fly back and forth. When she asserts that he owes her money, he tells her that Bardolph owes money too; let them coin his face, his nose, his cheeks (they are red, hence like copper). He is outraged at having his pocket picked in his own inn; he has lost a seal-ring of his grandfather's worth at least forty marks. The hostess claims that the Prince told her it was only a copper ring, and Sir John retorts that the Prince "is a Jack, a sneak-cup," and if he were here he would cudgel him like a dog.

The Prince and Poins suddenly enter, in marching stride, and Falstaff meets them playing on his truncheon (a short heavy stick or club) like a fife. He asks them if that is the way the wind is blowing; will they soon be marching? Bardolph interrupts sarcastically, "Yea, two and two, Newgate fashion" (that is, like prisoners). Falstaff tries to turn the Prince's attention to the picking of his pockets and the ring he has lost, but Hal pooh-poohs it as a trifling "eight-penny matter." The hostess now informs on Sir John, telling the Prince the vile insults he has offered him in his absence and of his threat to cudgel him. She swears by her "faith, truth, [and] womanhood" that she is speaking truly, and Falstaff bursts out, "There's no more faith in three than a stewed prune; nor no more truth in thee than in a drawn fox; and for womanhood, Maid Marianpmay be the deputy's wife of the ward to thee. Go, you thing, go."

Comment

These passes between Falstaff and the hostess seem the least intrinsic to the play of any of the witty dialogues thus far. And while they do serve, as here, to emphasize in yet another context the ideas of faith and truth, it seems that their chief function is to allow more witty sallies by Falstaff.

The Hostess is clearly a pawn for Falstaff. No match for him, she nevertheless continues to badger him. What kind of a "thing" does he mean, she asks. He replies, "a thing to thank God on," and she does not know quite how to take this but, perceiving vaguely that insult is intended, she denies it. She is an "honest man's wife"; and he is a "knave" to call her these things. He then retorts (setting her "womanhood" aside) that she is a beast. What beast? An otter. Why an otter? Because she's "neither fish nor flesh; a man knows not where to have her." The Prince defends her, saying that Falstaff is slandering her outrageously. The hostess matches this by replying that Falstaff has slandered the Prince also, by alleging that he owes him a thousand pounds. In anger (or pretended anger) Hal demands, "Do I owe you a thousand pound?" To which Falstaff, with his amiable dexterity of mind, answers: "A thousand pound, Hal? A million. Thy love is worth a million; thou owest me thy love." To all Falstaff's other boasts, the Prince challenges, "Dar'st thou be as good as thy word now?" Falstaff, of course, backs away from the challenge, but manages it with his accustomed ingenuity. As Hal is a man he dares to meet him, but as he is a prince he fears him-fears him as the "roaring of the lion's whelp." To Hal's question.", "And why not as the lion?" Falstaff replies, "The King himself is to be feared as the lion."

Comment

The image of the lion continues to appear in the play with such frequency that it begins to take on the status of a symbol.

The Hostess has a brief moment of triumph as the Prince hurls a spate of abuse at the fat knight: "there's no room for faith, truth, nor honesty in this bosom of thine; it is filed up with guts and midriff.... thou whoreson, impudent, embossed [swollen] rascal, if there were anything in thy pocket but tavern-reckonings, memorandums and bawdy-houses, and one poor penny-worth of sugar-candy to make thee long-winded ... I am a villain; and yet you will not stand to it; you will not pocket up wrong. Art thou not ashamed?"

Comment

Falstaff's answer is another monument to his wit, and to his ability, even at the most unlikely times, to elicit even genuine pathos for his own sort of "honesty." He says: "Dost thou hear, Hal? Thou knowest in the state of innocency Adam fell; and what should poor Jack Falstaff do in the days of villainy? Thou seest I have more flesh than another man, and therefore more frailty." (The idea of the "frailty of the flesh" refers to flesh in the general sense of "body as opposed to soul," but Falstaff wittily accommodates it to his "flesh," or girth.

With amazing aplomb, Falstaff says to the hostess, "I forgive thee." And he dispatches her to go about her household duties. He then turns to the Prince for a serious account of the news at court.

The Prince informs him that the money has been paid back, and that he is now on good terms with his father. Falstaff tries to continue in a lighthearted vein, joking about Hal's robbing the treasury, but the Prince will not be drawn into humorous flights of wit. He tells Falstaff forthrightly that he has gotten command of a troop of foot soldiers. Falstaff wishes it had been a troop of cavalry (horse), but he claims to welcome the opportunity. The Prince sends Bardolph with a letter to his brother, Lord John of Lancaster, and another to Westmoreland. To Poins he says, "Go Poins, to horse, to horse; for thou and I have thirty miles to ride yet ere dinner time." He directs Falstaff to meet him in the Temple Hall at two o'clock the following day, where he will be given money and orders for equipment.

Comment

There is an obvious no-nonsense air of command about the Prince as he peremptorily gives orders and barks instructions. We see his decision to gratify his father's wishes translated here into practical form.

As the scene closes, the young Prince exits on a stirring rhyming **couplet**, and Falstaff trumpets another on its heels:

[Prince] "The land is burning; Percy stands on high; And either they or we must lower lie." [Exit] [Falstaff] "Rare words! brave world! Hostess, my breakfast, come! O, I could wish this tavern were my drum!" [Exit]

Comment

The ultimate "rejection of Falstaff" is nowhere better prefigured than in this juxtaposition of lines. For one thing, the rhyming is couplet usually spoken by a noble character to mark the end of a scene, and it is frequently as expression of some lofty purpose, as indeed Hal's is. His words epitomize his altered purpose. But Falstaff's words show clearly that he remains a static character. There is some sincerity to his remark, but by being a **parody** of the Prince's exit line, they show Falstaff's inability to rise to a new occasion. It is perhaps at this point that we begin to take the satirical Falstaffian undercurrent not so much as an ironic comment on noble pretense, but as a symbol of the essentially limited vision of the world he represents. Falstaff stands for an element in human nature that must be faced, that is more good than bad, but which is not the highest good, and which can be evil when it becomes permanently destructive of social order.

SUMMARY

After the crisis (or turning point) in Act III, Scene 2, we might expect the action to take a more rapid turn, and indeed this is exactly what happens in this scene. Our understanding of the character of the Prince and of Falstaff is also greatly increased. Some important aspects of this are:

1. The Prince demonstrates both in his courteous treatment of the hostess and in his take-charge attitude toward Bardolph, Poins, and Falstaff that he is clearly in command of the situation and in control of himself. From this point on, dramatically speaking, there is no possibility that he will fail to fulfill his destiny in the play.

2. Falstaff's behavior illustrates that just the opposite is true of him. It is not that he degenerates in any way, or that his marvelous wit ever fails him, but that our deeper understanding of the real issues facing the Prince is a kind of unmasking of Falstaff for us.

3. Action: the Prince has made (or will soon make) all necessary preparations to field an army. Falstaff is given command of an infantry troop.

4. Falstaff's mock repentance and his jibes at Bardolph's red face still draw a laugh, but as satirical reflections of a main "action" they have lost some of their punch.

5. Repetition of thematic language and **imagery** is slight, except for:

    a. some by-play on "faith" and "truth"

    b. brief mention of the "lion" and "horse" figures.

6. The minor characters, Bardolph and the Hostess, appear here in greater depth than previously.

HENRY IV, PART 1

TEXTUAL ANALYSIS

ACT IV

ACT IV: SCENE 1

Act IV is the shortest act of the play. The first scene opens at the rebel camp near Shrewsbury, and things are happening very rapidly. Hotspur and Douglas, who are very much alike, are conversing, and Hotspur compliments Douglas by remarking that "not a soldier of this season's stamp" goes so "general current through the world," using once more his war coinage metaphor. Douglas repays the compliment, calling young Percy the "king of honor." A messenger enters with letters from the Earl of Northumberland, who reports that he is "grievous sick" and cannot lead his forces into battle. Hotspur is incredulous at the news, and comments that "this sickness doth infect. The very life-blood of our enterprise."

Comment

Northumberland's actual sickness (or it may be feigned sickness) mirrors the King's earlier "sickness' (he was "shaken ... and wan with care") over the civil disturbance and his son's waywardness; it is a way of suggesting that they have in fact symbolically changed places-something Henry has unwittingly anticipated with his wish to have Hotspur for a son instead of Hal.

The Earl has informed them, however, that they must proceed. There is no stopping now. Hotspur, with characteristic verve, quickly recovers from this blow. He refuses to take the Earl's illness as a sign of their certain defeat, to forecast the outcome "on the nice hazard of one doubtful hour." Douglas agrees, and remarks that they should think instead of their future victory and rewards. Worcester, a more reserved and cautious man, is disturbed over the effect this news will have on the armies; for they cannot afford the slightest suggestion of a lack of agreement among the leaders of the rebellion. Some might easily imagine that the Earl's absence is the result of some private reservations about the wisdom of their plan. This is especially dangerous for the "offering" (that is, the rebellious) side. They must stop up all such loopholes before the news begins to breed fear in the soldiers.

Hotspur tells him that he is making a mountain out of molehill. In fact, the Earl's absence gives their enterprise a greater aspect of daring-a greater luster. There is more "honor" to be gained by it. All is yet well. Douglas concurs, adding, "There is not such a word / Spoke of in Scotland as this term of fear."

Comment

This sort of national partisan pride we see in Douglas, as well as the former disputes between Percy and Glendower (at least to the extent that they were motivated by national differences) does not augur well for the outcome of the war. This is a basic "division" of spirit among the rebels, and Worcester has just remarked that their enterprise "brooks no division."

Sir Richard appears with the news that Westmoreland and Prince John are marching toward them, and that the King himself is on the verge of setting out. Hotspur embraces the challenge with another scornful dismissal of the Prince of Wales, though he asks Vernon for news of him. Vernon's speech in reply is one of the most ironic touches in this act for, in spite of himself, he describes the Prince in glowing terms, in imaginative martial language, the only sort of language that makes any sense to Hotspur. He rose, says Vernon, "from the ground like feathered Mercury,/ And vaulted with such ease unto his seat, As if an angel dropp'd down from the clouds." Hotspur is visibly shaken by Vernon's words, and he cries out, "No more, no more!"

But again Percy recovers, and with an almost maniacal defiance he welcomes the royalist armies as sacrifices marching to the altar of the God of War, to whom they will offer them "all hot and bleeding." Mars will sit on his altar, up to his ears in blood. And the twinlike relationship of the two cousins comes out emphatically in the **couplet**: "Harry to Harry shall, hot horse to horse, Meet, and ne'er part till one drop down a corse" (corse means corpse).

Vernon has even worse news. Glendower has not been able to muster his forces. Even Douglas is disturbed at this, but Hotspur rises to another romantic pitch, crying out, "Come, let us take a muster speedily./Doomsday is near. Die all, die merrily." All leave.

SUMMARY

This is a short scene with much action.

1. We learn (from the rebels' viewpoint) of several important developments:

    a. Northumberland is out of action.

    b. Westmoreland and Prince John are on the march.

    c. The King is equipped and ready to move.

    d. The Prince of Wales has emerged as an impressive general (at least in appearance - the way he bestrides a horse - and this is enough to impress Hotspur).

2. We see the first real shaking of Hotspur's confidence, though not his determination.

3. The personalities of several characters emerge more fully as they contribute to the action:

    a. Douglas is seen as spirited, but somewhat narrow-minded.

> b. Worcester's calm persuasive manner is exercised again, but to no avail-Hotspur will join in combat anyway.
>
> c. Sir Richard Vernon appears in a somewhat favorable light.

All of these characters, in one way or another, tend to throw into relief the character of Hotspur, The rebels, taken as a whole, do not make a bad showing, but we come to feel that "division" is of the very nature of rebellion. No individual qualities of mind will suffice to make them successful against an "anointed king." (The fact that Henry himself was a successful rebel has much to do with the fact that Richard had himself sinned against his crown.)

ACT IV: SCENE 2

This very brief scene begins with Falstaff and Bardolph on a public road near Coventry. Falstaff sends Bardolph off for a bottle of sack and then delivers one of his most impressive soliloquies- amusing, but tinged with pathos. He reveals that he has misused his power of conscription by letting able-bodied men who had enough money buy draft exemptions. He had sought out only those with a good reason for wanting to remain on the home front-landowners, bachelors about to be married, out-and- out cowards -and summoned them. Pocketing the money he then filled up his company with all the broken-down relics of humanity he could find, "the cankers of a calm world and a long peace." One would think he had a hundred and fifty prodigals straight from their swine-keeping; one mad fellow on the road told Sir John that it looked as though he had unloaded all the gallows and pressed all the dead bodies into service. They look either like scarecrows or ex-convicts.

Comment

This view of the seamier side of war contrasts markedly with the lofty mouthings we have heard from Hotspur and Douglas in the last scene.

Prince and Westmoreland enter, and after a brief humorous exchange Hal remarks that he has never seen such "pitiful rascals." Falstaff's rejoinder is memorable for its combination of profundity and casualness-it one of the truly affecting and penetrating utterances in the play; even the possibility that Falstaff is posing as he speaks cannot spoil it: "Tut, tut; good enough to toss; food for powder, food for powder; they'll fill a pit as well as better; tush, man, mortal men, mortal men." The Prince bids Falstaff make haste, for Percy is already in the field.

SUMMARY

These brief scenes, which move us back and forth from the rebel to the royalist side, catch some of the helter-skelter motion of the moment. The sense of action and urgency is pointed up. This scene also anticipates, in its juxtaposition of Hotspur's exalted sentiments and Falstaff's ragged band, the ultimate confrontation on the battlefield of Hotspur and Falstaff, and the final confrontation of the ideal order of things each stands for. It should be noted, too, that the vague tens of thousands that Hotspur alludes to so airily are matched by the few pitiful specimens so vividly described by Sir John.

ACT IV: SCENE 3

We are back at the rebel camp. Hotspur, Worcester, Douglas, and Vernon enter. They are obviously on edge, and they speak in clipped, nervous phrases. Douglas accuses Vernon of fear, and Vernon warns him that he will meet slander with a fight to the death, if necessary; his reply also suggests that Douglas has been getting on their nerves with his talk about the bravery of the Scots. Vernon tries to keep a level head, and he rebukes Hotspur and Douglas for not realizing that their men and horses are tired and that certain reinforcements have not yet arrived. But Hotspur wants to press the fight. Worcester, too, pleads with him not to engage the superior numbers of the enemy, but to wait for the remainder of their army.

A trumpet sounds for a parley, and Sir Walter Blunt enters. He speaks with dignity and restraint. And Hotspur compliments him, telling him that there are those among them who wish he were ranged with the rebels against the King. Blunt, however, makes the steadfast answer that he will stand against them as an enemy, "So long as out of limit and true rule / You stand against anointed majesty."

Comment

Blunt has been the prime example in the play, of a king's faithful servitor. Hotspur's flattery and his later explanation of their complaint against Henry carry absolutely no weight with him. Henry is an anointed king, a fact which removes him from the arena of personal spites and grievances.

Blunt conveys the King's gracious offer to listen to their complaints, his generous promise of redress for their grief, and full pardon for themselves and their followers. But if there had ever been a chance for Hotspur to change his course of action, that time is long past. He speaks disparagingly of Henry when he had just returned from exile as "a poor unminded outlaw sneaking home," and he describes the assistance his father the Earl had given him and how all the lords and barons of the country had flocked to his side, following Northumberland's example. He goes on to analyze what he considers the hypocritical acts of Bolingbroke which won the people's hearts; he ends by noting sarcastically that Henry did not stop at hearts, he

> "Proceeded further; cut me off the heads Of all the favorites that the absent king In deputation left behind him here, When he was personal in the Irish war."

Comment

This may well be the point at which the numerous references to "head" in the play clearly appear as a basic figure or concept. "Head" can mean (among many other things):

1. the human head

2. the mind as opposed to the heart

3. the obverse side of a coin

4. the ruler of a kingdom

5. a force raised up in insurrection (a rebel army)

6. virginity (in the word "maidenhead")

The King's crowned head, the rebel army, the head of the land considered as a "body," the heads on the coins punned on so frequently, Bardolph's head, the "maidenheads" which the Prince jokes about purchasing so cheaply, the heads which Hotspur here accuses the King of having cut off, the "head in the noose" (another kind of circled, or "crowned" head), the "crack'd crowns," and probably several other "heads" all enter into a general complex of symbolism. One of the most important aspects of this symbolism is the way in which some of these minor "heads," which are in a fair way to be lost, tent to mirror the potential danger of the state's losing its head.

Hotspur now recites a long list of particular acts of the King, directed against the Percies. After deposing Richard and having him murdered, Henry:

1. left Mortimer to languish in Wales without ransom

2. disgraced Hotspur even in his moment of victory

3. had Hotspur spied upon

4. gave Worcester a tongue-lashing and removed him from the council

5. dismissed the Earl of Northumberland from the court

6. broke "oath upon oath," and committed "wrong on wrong"

7. (this is the vaguest of all) "drove us to seek out this head of safety" and to "pry into his title" (that is, to reexamine the whole question on Henry's legitimate claim to the throne)

Blunt asks if he should return this answer to the King, and Hotspur (in a surprising show of caution) tells him to wait. Worcester will bring their answer in the morning.

SUMMARY

1. The rebels are sniping at one another, and it is clear that they are worried. What is more, their forces are tired and outnumbered.

2. The essential rightness of the King's position is symbolized by the dignified presence of Sir Walter Blunt.

3. We are given a clear statement of the rebels' grievances (actually, for the first time).

4. The implications of Henry's status as an "anointed majesty" are made clear and brought into connection with the head-crown **imagery**. Henry, as "head" of the kingdom, is opposed by a "head" - the rebel army.

ACT IV: SCENE 4

This exceptionally brief scene takes place at the palace of the Archbishop of York. The Archbishop is dispatching a friend, called only Sir Michael, with letters to unspecified persons urging their support of Hotspur's cause. All we really learn is that Owen Glendower's absence is due to his being "overruled by prophecies," and the Scroop (the Archbishop) is in a panic. There is a slight touch of **irony** in his reference to the rebel leaders as a "head of gallant warriors" when it is immediately followed by a reference to the King's party as "the special head of all the land." Principally, the scene accomplishes two things:

1. It anticipates the defeat of the rebel army.

2. It creates the illusion of a lapse of time between the conference of Blunt and Hotspur, and the dawning of the day of battle.

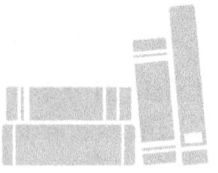

HENRY IV, PART 1

TEXTUAL ANALYSIS

ACT V

ACT V: SCENE 1

The Fifth Act brings all the groups together on the stage and weaves together the various thematic strands which have threaded through the separate but analogous careers of the rebels, the rioters, and the royalists. The first scene is set in the King's camp near Shrewsbury. The King, Prince Henry, Prince John, Falstaff, and Blunt are present. Henry and the Prince comment on the ominous appearance of the bloody morning sun and the southern wind. A trumpet sounds, and Worcester and Vernon enter with their answer. The King rebukes Worcester as an "exhaled meteor, a prodigy of fear," and asks when he will "move in that obedient orb again / Where you did give a fair and natural light" (tying together once more the images of nature and order). Worcester adopts a somewhat wheedling tone, in his recital of grievances-a catalogue of complaints which is hardly different from what Hotspur has already said. Worcester, however, concentrates on the fact that Henry has violated his oath to them (he repeats this several times), and he says that "you yourself have forged [means] against yourself / By unkind usage, dangerous countenance,. / And violation of all faith and troth."

Comment

This is perhaps the most important instance of the "faith and truth" figure. Worcester implicitly defends their revolt on the grounds that Henry has forfeited their allegiance by his "unkindness" (which means, primarily, "unnaturalness"), and his violation of faith, both of which are actions unbecoming a king.

Worcester also portrays Henry's ingratitude in an image which reverberates with echoes of Falstaff's limitless appetite and thus helps to provide a unifying dimension for the two plots. He says that Henry, like the cuckoo,

> "... did oppress our nest; Grew by our feeding to so great a bulk That even our love durst not come near your sight For fear of swallowing ... "

But the King, with dignified contempt, dismisses Worcester's charges as the specious reasons of a wanton rebel. Hal then throws an open challenge to the absent Hotspur, praising him as a valiant, daring, and bold gentleman, but offering to meet him in single combat. Henry refuses to allow this, on the ground that "considerations infinite do make against it."

Comment

This rather vague excuse may simply reflect Henry's relief that the Prince has justified his right of succession, and his fear of risking the future king's life unnecessarily.

Henry displays his true royalty by refusing to bargain, even while he offers his free and unconditional pardon.

The Prince and Falstaff are left alone on stage, and Falstaff complains, "I wouldn't were bed-time, Hal, and all well." To which the Prince retorts, Why thou owest God a death," and exits, leaving Falstaff to deliver his famous soliloquy on honor. Can honor set a broken arm or leg or take away the pain of a wound? No. Then it has no skill in surgery. Honor is a mere word, and a word is nothing but air. Who has it? The dead hero. But can he feel it or hear it? No. It is therefore insensible to the dead, but can it live with the living? No. Why? Envy will not allow it to. "Therefore I'll none of it."

SUMMARY

There are some extraordinarily long speeches in this scene, which do not really advance the plot. But they help to solve the dramatic problem of presenting a war on stage. Obviously, a realistic war is out of the question, but there is a kind of substitute for it in the confrontation of Worcester and the King. The quality of the speeches, as well as the substance of their arguments, results in one conclusion: "majesty" vanquishes "rebellion." Thus, they carry on a kind of symbolic battle of Shrewsbury. There are, in addition, these minor functions:

1. All the earlier forms of "faith and truth" are reflected in the main plot in Worcester's accusation of faithlessness against Henry. (Ironically, he returns and fails to tell the "truth" to Hostspur.)

2. The image of "feeding to excess" is applied to Henry, who thus sustains a brief comparison with Falstaff.

3. The Prince appears in his most generous and noble guise so far.

ACT V: SCENE 2

We are shown the rebel camp again. Worcester is informing Vernon of his decision not to tell Hotspur of the King's generous offer of truce. Worcester's explanation is one more illustration of the idea than rebellion causes noble minds to degenerate. From a cautious dignified gentleman, Worcester is seen to descend to the level of a defensive, suspicious, and mendacious man. He will not give Hotspur the true word because he is afraid Hotspur might accept the terms, and that Henry will later exact some form of retribution from Northumberland and himself, even while excusing Hotspur for his "youth and heat of blood." So he and Vernon tell Hotspur and Douglas that there was no mercy in the King. Westmoreland, who had been held as a hostage pending their safe return, is released to return their challenge to Henry. Worcester does report accurately the challenge that the Prince has offered, and Hotspur, whose own character is becoming more and more infected with choler and suspicion, asks how the challenge was delivered: "Seemed it in contempt?"

Comment

The fact is that Hal's offer of single combat was couched in most gracious terms, a fact which Vernon elaborates on with such gusto that Hotspur accuses him of being "enamoured" on the follies of the Prince. The more "nobility" Hal shows, the more petty Hotspur seems to grow. This is of course one of the results of Hotspur's dramatic function as foil to the Prince.

Young Percy defies the Prince and announces that he will "embrace him with a soldier's arm." He calls for speed in arming and shunts aside a messenger with a letter because there is not time:

> "O gentlemen, the time of life is short! To spend that shortness basely were too long, If life did ride upon a dial's point, Still ending at the arrival of an hour."

Comment

The whole question of "time" in the play is an important one. This speech looks back to Hal's very first remarks about there being no need for Falstaff to worry about time unless "dials were signs of leaping-houses" and so forth. Time is almost a tangible commodity. It is compressed into an instant for Hotspur, expanded out of existence for Falstaff; the Prince thinks of his conversion in terms of "redeeming time when men think least I will."

Percy commands "all the lofty instruments of war" to be sounded. The rebel leaders embrace. Trumpets sound, and they leave the stage.

HENRY IV, PART 1

SUMMARY

This scene accomplishes only a few things beyond establishing the rebels' irreversible defiance.

1. The character of Worcester is seen at its worst - the implication being that this is the ultimate fate of any conspirator. He even speaks of Hotspur's faults as "corruption."

2. The sincerity of the Prince's new "nobility" and "courtesy" can be seen in the fact that even his enemy Vernon is quite swept away by it.

ACT V: SCENE 3

The long-anticipated battle has finally materialized. The scene is a plain between the camps, and the king's army crosses the stage. Douglas and Sir Walter Blunt then enter.

Comment

Douglas challenges Blunt, who is disguised in the King's livery. We find out a little later that several knights have been disguises as the King. This can be taken as one more point of comparison between Falstaff and Henry. Falstaff "counterfeits" death as Henry "counterfeits" living images of himself. (It is in the next scene, of course, that Falstaff "plays dead.")

Blunt proudly refuses to yield to Douglas' challenge. They fight and Blunt is killed. Hotspur enters briefly and tells

Douglas about the disguised knights, whereupon he threatens to "murder all his wardrobe, piece by piece." They leave and Falstaff appears, alone. We find out that he has led his men into the thick of it; there are not more than three left alive from three hundred and fifty. The Prince now arrives on the scene, rebukes Falstaff for standing idle, and asks to borrow his sword. Sir John offers him his pistol, but when Hal takes it from the case he finds it contains only a bottle of sack. Crying, "What, is it a time to jest and dally now?" he throws it at Falstaff and leaves. Sir John comments that he does not like the kind of "grinning honor" that Sir Walter Blunt has. "Give me life," he cries. The scene ends.

SUMMARY

This scene is another counterpointing of the serious and the comic aspects of honor.

1. Blunt chooses honor, though faced by a superior foe, and dies, presumably happy in the choice that he has made.

2. Falstaff, sneaking away from the fight, stumbles upon Blunt. The bottle of sack in his pistol case in his solution to the problem of honor, and we can presume that he is also happy in his choice.

3. Falstaff's remarks about the kind of "honor" Blunt has, shows that the two men inhabit different planes of existence. Blunt's code is not Falstaff's, and the implication certainly is that life has to be broad enough to find room for both.

ACT V: SCENE 4

Scene four shows us another part of the field. The King, the Prince, Lord John, and Westmoreland enter amidst confused sallies and trumpet calls. The Prince is wounded but refuses to retire. His brother John, impatient for action, returns to the battle and Hal remarks with surprise on his newly matured courage. Westmoreland and the Prince both exit, leaving Henry alone, and Douglas enters and engages the King in a duel. The King is being hard pressed when Hal returns and puts Douglas to flight. Henry acknowledges that this shows that the Prince has some concern for his life, to which Hal replies: "O God! they did me too much injury / That ever said I hearken'd for your death" (this is one of the unspoken bones of contention between the King and his son-Henry's suspicion that Hal was conspiring to overthrow him). The King exits. Hotspur enters. They challenge each other: The Prince, graciously; Hotspur, boastfully. They fight, and the Prince kills Percy, who makes a dying speech in which he bemoans the loss of his "proud titles" more than the loss of his life. While they have been fighting, Falstaff and Douglas have come in. No sooner have they crossed swords than Falstaff falls on the ground playing dead (Douglas, of course, leaves). The Prince now makes a speech over the dead body of Percy which gains an ironic emphasis from the fact that the "dead" body of Falstaff is lying nearby.

Comment

For one thing, the Prince remarks, "This earth that bears thee dead / Bears not alive so stout a gentleman." There is an unintended pun on "stout," meaning both "courageous" and "corpulent"; in the first sense it applies to Percy, in the second (though Hal is not aware of it), it applies to Falstaff. There is a problem here for the actor: Should Falstaff play it broadly, sitting up and winking (behind Hal's back) at the audience, or should he simply lie there motionless?

The Prince suddenly spies the body of Falstaff lying on the ground, and he makes an equivalent speech over his body, the main purport of which is expressed in the **couplet**: "O, I should have a heavy miss of thee / If I were much in love with vanity." The Prince leaves, and Falstaff rises up and makes another of his famous soliloquies, this time on "counterfeiting." If he had not counterfeited, Douglas would have killed him. But who is truly the counterfeit? It is the dead man, for he is only the counterfeit of a man. Therefore, to counterfeit death is to preserve the "true and perfect image of life itself." He decides to pretend that he himself killed Percy, so he stabs him in the thigh and raises the dead body up on his back. The Prince and his brother enter, astonished to hear Falstaff's claim that he himself killed Hotspur. They were both down and out of breath, he says, but they rose and "fought a long hour by Shrewsbury clock." The Prince, in good humor, says, "Come, bring your luggage nobly on your back. / For my part, if a lie may do thee grace, / I'll gild it with the happiest terms I have." All leave.

SUMMARY

This scene shows us the sharpest differentiation so far between the points of view represented by Hotspur and Falstaff, and it presents this distinction in very concrete terms. At the same time, the Prince's speeches make it clear that he is completely out from under the influence of Falstaff and the shadow of Hotspur. Other points made are:

1. The King has also practiced a kind of "counterfeiting."

> 2. Even for Hotspur, "honor" has become a matter of "proud titles"; Blunt, if anyone, seems to remain the most balanced example of genuine honor and chivalry.

ACT V: SCENE 5

The final scene of the play ties up the remaining loose ends. The rebels have been subdued and prisoners taken. The King sentences Worcester and Vernon to death, but leaves the disposition of Douglas to the Prince, Hal magnanimously frees him - and without ransom - as a reward for the example of his valor.

Comment

This shows that Hal has not rejected completely the ideal espoused by Hotspur. Hotspur was simply an extreme expression of it.

Prince John has been given the duty of informing Douglas, and he thanks his brother for his "high courtesy."

Comment

After all the limitations of "courtesy" have been exposed, it is nevertheless reestablished as a necessary kingly attribute.

Henry issues new commands to the armies, since Northumberland, Scroop, and Glendower are still at large, and he puts into words what has been the main them of the play on both levels (the Prince given over to "riot," and the Percies given over to revolt): "Rebellion in this land shall lose his sway."

Comment

As it customary in history plays, the King is the last to speak. His two rhyming **couplets** give an edge of formality and ceremony to the ending.

SUMMARY

The war ends, the rebels are punished, valor is rewarded, and the main action of the play is pointedly underlined as a thing which has been completed. The "putting down of rebellion" (in the nation, the family, and the individual) has been successfully achieved.

HENRY IV, PART 1

CHARACTER ANALYSES

KING HENRY

The King is a strong shrewd politician and a capable warrior. He has usurped the throne and has had Richard murdered and, when the play opens, is suffering the results of the civil dissension which followed these violent acts. He is haunted by the fear that his oldest son, who should succeed him to the throne, will be the same kind of wastrel that Richard was, and he is distraught to think that Northumberland's son Henry (Hotspur) is more truly "honorable" and worthy of the throne than Hal. There is a touch of hypocrisy in Henry (as he glosses over the extent of his moral fault), and a tinge of vanity (seen in the boastful reminiscences of his youth in the conversation with Hal). We feel that Worcester's suspicion that he will never be able to trust Henry may be justified. But he has the poise and the address of a king-a necessary coldness and a peremptory attitude.

PRINCE HENRY

Prince Henry (Harry or Hal) is something of a chip off the old block. He is likeable enough, but there is a calculating quality in his nature which is a disturbing undertone to the frequent generosity he displays. But it remains an undertone only and is a reminder that a king, after all, is not a commoner. He has been exploring the varieties of human excess and riot by hobnobbing with Falstaff, Poins, and the other cut-purses, but we are never really in doubt of his eventual reform. When the chips are down, his salad days are abruptly terminated. He promises his father obedience and faith and makes good on them. He fights valiantly, treats his enemies with chivalry, and (in the case of Douglas) shows true princely generosity by freeing him with no strings attached. The stumbling block to interpretation of his character is the opening soliloquy in which he speaks of hanging around with Falstaff and the other tavern-haunters only so he will appear more laudable in people's eyes when he does reform.

MINOR SUPPORTERS OF THE KING

Westmoreland is the very image of the trusted counselor; Blunt, of the valiant defender. They are both absolutely loyal to Henry, and Blunt dies valiantly at Douglas' hand. Their loyalty is stressed as a marked antithesis to the faithlessness of the Percies. Prince John, who appears only late in the play, is seen as a young man who is just maturing into a brave soldier and a capable leader.

NORTHUMBERLAND

The Earl does not really figure prominently in the play. He is courteous enough to the King when he speaks to him, and he is calm and reasonable in dealing with Hotspur. But his disloyalty to the King, and his consequent degeneration of character is seen to result in the rather transparent excuse he offers for not taking part in the battle at Shrewsbury.

HOTSPUR

Young Henry Percy is a peculiar combination of valor and choler. He is the ideal chivalric knight in extreme form. His life is so ordered on the principle of combat at all costs that he lacks real discrimination. We see in him how easily valor can turn to pugnaciousness, and honor into the empty clutching of proud titles. His death at the Prince's hands is the only fitting conclusion for him.

MORTIMER

The Earl of March is not shown off to good advantage in the play. There is a suggestion of a too-willing compromise in his wielding to Glendower, and there is somewhat of a simpering tone to his complaints about his unfortunate inability to converse with his wife. As a potential king he is never really in the running, and Shakespeare's emphasis on his ineffectualness is one more way of underlining the legitimacy of Henry's reign.

GLENDOWER

Glendower is something of an oddity. He has freakish interests and is moved by imponderable occult motives. Thh Percies' alliance with him is a kind of symbol of the fact that their violations of "order" put them into association with the "unnatural" in human affairs.

DOUGLAS

Douglas is the courageous but boastful warrior, proud of his flag, but lacking in real imagination. He does fit well, however, into a strictly ordered society, and his pardon at the end of the play may be a symbol on this fact.

WORCESTER

Worcester is the cautious self-seeking politician. He is under no illusions about the dangers he faces, and he knows Henry well. There is a clear suggestion that participation in rebellion has caused caution and self-interest to turn to perfidy in his case. But he accepts his fate stoically, without begging or whining.

MINOR ADHERENTS TO THE PERCY CAUSE

Vernon is an impressionable man, a victim of circumstances who is easily led and who might, with a hairbreadth change of circumstances, have been on the royalist side. He is a brave man, however, and essentially level-headed. Scroop (the Archbishop) appears very briefly, and when he does he is making friends for himself against the coming day of retribution. (Sir Michael is clearly an underling of no importance.)

FALSTAFF

"O, for words to utter what is like thee!" How can one sum up the character of Falstaff? Objectively, we can describe him: gourmand, toss-pot, thief, liar, master of wit. Subjectively considered, he is an enigma. All attempts to answer the question of cowardice in any final way are doomed. The fact is that he stands not for a particular man, or type of man, but for an aspect of human nature which will not submit to moral judgments. He is the healthy side of appetite; he is human vitality without respect to moral sanctions. He is the perennially appearing spirit of release from restraint which the young Prince must face up to but must eventually overcome if he is to wear the crown.

FALSTAFF'S COMPANIONS

Poins, the Prince's favorite friend, is a man of understanding and sensibility. The rest, Bardolph, Peto, and Gadshill, are undiscriminated types from the underside of London society.

THE LADIES

Kate, Hotspur's wife, is tender and has a sense of humor. She is grieving and somewhat annoyed at Hotspur's departure, but she bears it well. Mortimer's wife does not speak English in the play. From Glendower's translation, we learn that she has a tender affection for her husband. The hostess of the Boar's Head Tavern is tough and tender by turns. She submits to a good deal of bullying and rough language, but she will not take any slurs on her "honesty."

HENRY IV, PART 1

CRITICAL COMMENTARY

Henry IV, Part One has always been one of the most popular of Shakespeare's plays, probably largely because of that magnificent creation, Falstaff. Like *Hamlet*, he can be a challenge and a triumph for an actor. Even literary criticism of the play has tended to concentrate on Falstaff, following a long tradition which may be said to begin in the eighteenth century with Samuel Johnson. For Johnson, the Prince is a "young man of great abilities and violent passions," and Percy is a "rugged soldier," but "Falstaff, unimitated, unimitable Falstaff, how shall I describe thee? Thou compound of sense and vice … a character loaded with faults, and with faults which naturally produce contempt … a thief, a glutton, a coward, and a boaster, always ready to cheat the weak and prey upon the poor; to terrify the timorous the insult and defenseless … his wit is not of the splendid or ambitious kind, but consists in easy escapes and sallies of levity [yet] he is stained with no enormous or sanguinary crimes, so that his licentiousness is not so offensive but that it may be borne for his mirth."

There are three assumptions Johnson makes (perhaps any eighteenth-century critic would make) in his reading of the play that criticism has been wrestling with ever since:

1. That Falstaff is the kind of character who invites a moral or psychological judgment-principally, that he can answer to the charge of being a coward.

2. That the "mirth" of Falstaff (or of any Shakespearean clown, for that matter) is finally detachable from the plays and can exist for its own sake apart from the major **theme** of the drama. To put it another way, there are those who feel that Falstaff's long speeches and soliloquies are mere wit, and do not enter into a philosophical pattern of meaning in the play.

3. That the "slighter occurrences are diverting," that is, that the play is "really about" the fate of the kingdom, and that the tavern scenes are not intrinsically connected with the main action. What this comes down to is a denial that the play, as a whole, has any real unity.

About ten years later, Maurice Morgann composed a long semi-serious Essay on the Dramatic Character of Sir John Falstaff, in which he set out to prove that Falstaff was in fact not a "constitutional coward," but that having ordered his life on a principle of "wit and humor" all his actions had to be judged in this light. His fictitious death on the Shrewsbury battlefield is not cowardice, but simple a renunciation of the "tyranny of honor," a concept which he could observe only in a ridiculous light. In the process of defending Falstaff, Morgann ranged far beyond the details of personality provided by Shakespeare and constructed a complete, though hypothetical, biography for Sir John.

The concept of dramatic characters as really existing total human beings appealed also to the romantics, of whom Hazlitt is representative. For him, "Falstaff's wit is an emanation of a fine constitution; an exuberance of good humor ... and if he were not so fat as he is he would not be in character ... He manures and nourishes his mind with jests, as he does his body with sack and sugar." Hazlitt adds that "he keeps up perpetual holiday and open house ... yet we are not to suppose that he was a mere sensualist." The bottle of sack in his pistol case shows "his contempt for glory accompanied with danger"; and because he is old and fat "there is a melancholy retrospective tinge to his character."

A. C. Bradley, in his famous *Oxford Lecture* (1909) on the "Rejection of Falstaff" (referring to *Henry IV*, Part Two at the conclusion of which Hal, who has now become King, banishes Falstaff from his presence), undertakes once more to defend the fat knight against the charge of cowardice. In Bradley we see a progress away from mere acceptance of Falstaff's ignoble actions for the sake of his wit toward a view of him as a man who has "risen superior to all serious motives." In Georg Brandes' analysis of the play (1927) Falstaff is "a demi-god, supreme alike in intellect and wit." He "demonstrates in practice how a man can live without [honor], and we do not miss it in him, so perfect is he in his way." In the same year E. E. Stoll was renewing, with great vehemence and very close analysis of the text, the old charge of cowardice against Falstaff. The interesting thing about criticism of the play, from the beginnings through the first quarter of the twentieth century, is the almost exclusive interest in Falstaff, and the concentration on the question of his cowardice.

In the second quarter of this century, in the wake of the "new criticism, we find a broadening of interest, a much greater attention to other details of dramatic structure, such a **imagery** or the juxtaposition of scenes and characters. There has been a wealth of good criticism, of which only a few samples may be given: L. C. Knights, without minimizing the importance of

Falstaff, took the play as a **satire** on war and politics, a view in which the King came off badly. John Dover Wilson, perhaps the most renowned of modern critics of the play, took the very plausible position in his book, *The Fortunes of Falstaff* (1943), that the play is a version of the old morality-play **theme** of the Youth (Hal) who is tempted to vice and "riot" by a number of characters, chiefly Vanity (Falstaff), a tradition which finds a clear analogy in the biblical account of the prodigal son. The legend in this case has been slanted toward reformation in the sense of "fitness to rule" rather than simple moral reform, partly because of the contemporary interest in the Renaissance concept of the "ideal Prince." Wilson (like others) also allows for the influence of classical comedy as well, especially the stock figures of the "young wastrel" and the "braggart soldier."

E. M. W. Tillyard, in his *Shakespeare's History Plays* (1944), put forward the novel theory (which has not met with general acceptance) that Shakespeare, in *Richard II, Henry IV*, Part One, *Henry IV*, Part Two, and *Henry V*, was writing a kind of "dramatic epic," and that these plays make up a Lancastrian tetralogy. He finds a general concept of hierarchy and degree to be the basis for all four plays and sees interweaving motifs of "order" contributing to give the four plays an over-all unity. Cleanth Brooks and Robert Heilman in *Understanding Drama* (1945) make a painstaking analysis of the play in a "new critical" fashion and call attention to important verbal patterns and patterns of **imagery** which echo through the drama and serve to bind it into an esthetic whole. They also stress its function as a comedy rather than a history play and insist very reasonably on the necessity of an audience's accepting the ambiguous aspects of Falstaff's performance (indeed, the many ambiguities the play offers) as inherent in Shakespeare's theme-which, in fact, has to do with the complexity of human decisions as this becomes apparent to the young Prince.

As representative of the contributions made to our understanding of the play, by critics writing in the 1940s and early 1950s, we might mention: A. J. A. Waldock's "The Men in Buckram," in which the author points out a meaningful difference of texture (as well as location, action, purpose, and so forth) between the "upper-plot" and the "under-plot," requiring in the reader two mental attitudes and two sets of responses. Irving Ribner's "The Political Problem in Shakespeare's Lancastrian Tetralogy" (1952), stresses Shakespeare's sympathy with Bolingbroke's usurpation of the throne. He feels that Shakespeare condemned Bolingbroke's sin but not his reign and demonstrated in *Henry IV* that the ability to maintain order and restore the peace is finally more important than succession by "divine right." M. A. Shaaber, in 1947, attacked Wilson's and Tillyard's view that the two parts of *Henry IV* are a unity, showing that there is very little evidence to prove that any "two-part" plays in the Elizabethan period were ever performed in such a way as to suggest their unity to an audience and questioning whether, in any case, a "unified" two-part play is artistically superior to two casually linked plays. H. E. Cain in "Further Light on the Relations of 1 and 2 *Henry IV*" (1952) argues against the unity of the two plays on the plausible grounds that there are certain events and dramatic accomplishments in the first part which have been forgotten, and repeated in the second. G. H. Hunter answer this claim in his "*Henry IV* and the Elizabethan Two-part Play" 1954) by referring to Cain's points as objections against "continuity" rather than "unity." The two plays, he feels, have a unity of **theme** rather than of story.

Lily B. Campbell, in the influential book *Shakespeare's "Histories:" Mirrors of Elizabethan Policy* (1947), made an exhaustive analysis of the history plays as commentaries on contemporary political life. In *Henry IV* she finds Shakespeare was adapting "history to the teaching of the causes and results of rebellion," and she discovers a marked similarity between the Percies' revolt as Shakespeare presents it and the Northern Rebellion of 1569 (against Elizabeth).

Out of the numerous possibilities for analyzing literature which modern critical methods have made possible, several exciting approaches have been made to *Henry IV*, Part One. Two examples will suffice here. Derek Traversi (in *Shakespeare from Richard II to Henry IV* [1957]) illustrates brilliantly the results of close attention to symbolic detail. He finds an important part of the play's main conception to be "the tracing of a common destiny working itself out through character." Traversi's analysis of Falstaff emphasizes his status as a "foil" rather than a "temptation" to the Prince; Falstaff's combination of "warm, alert humanity" with "inherited Christian tradition," for example, sets off the cold, practical calculations of the Prince. C. L. Barber's study of the analogies to literary drama which can be discovered in folk ritual and which can illuminate the meaning of literature are stimulating indeed. Barber (in his "From Ritual to Comedy: An Examination of *Henry IV*" [1955], and in his later book, *Shakespeare's Festive Comedy* [1959], stresses the function of Falstaff as a lord of misrule. The result is that misrule is seen as "consolidating rule," for misrule (or Saturnalia) means a temporary abandonment to riot, with order and sanity following with renewed vitality.

Each age, each method, each set of values, calls forth new meaning from the plays (and from the character of Falstaff), and it is more than likely that criticism of the play will, in the future, increase rather than decline.

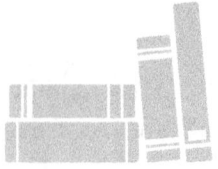

HENRY IV, PART 1

ESSAY QUESTIONS AND ANSWERS

Question: In what ways, and for what reasons, might Hotspur and Falstaff be regarded as "foils" to one another?

Answer: It is certainly no longer novel to remark that Hotspur and Falstaff represent alternative extremes for Prince Henry. Hotspur is the very embodiment of chivalry (in the beginning), and Falstaff is the embodiment of riotous behavior. But Hotspur is a "flat" character; there is no complexity to speak of in his vision of human life and its meaning. Falstaff is a "round" character. He is a constant commentary on the pretense of noble and "mannered" members of society. The many scenes in which he apes the (to him) antics of courtly conversation, horsemanship, or valorous conduct have their function as contrasts to the "noble" characters generally, but especially to Hostpur. It is no accident that they lie together on the battlefield, and that Hal makes equivalent speeches over their bodies. It is no accident, either, that Falstaff rises again, for he has proven that honor equals death, and that he is devoid of honor.

HENRY IV, PART 1

Question: Define the major **theme** of the play.

Answer: There can be no question that the play is concerned with the necessity for order, and that the action of the play involves the quelling of disturbance and the reestablishment of order. But the order takes different forms. For one thing, it is civil order, now threatened by the Percies. The kind of "honor" espoused by Hotspur, because it is not decently subordinated to feudal loyalty, grows out of all bound-becomes rebellion - and must be put down. But Falstaff's corpulence is also a failure of order, and it is the symbolic equivalent of the Prince's lack of ordered control of his own life. Even the farcical scenes, the carrier's complaints about the "disordered" inn, for example, repeat this idea. All the major characters, in their own ways, suffer some incapacity for their sins against order: Henry, wan with care; Falstaff, walking twelve paces as if it were a mile. They speak of reforming: the King, seriously (his trip to Jerusalem); Falstaff, mockingly (his intention to purge cleanly and leave sack). The Prince's problem can even be put as a problem in knowing how to face the necessity for order. How can he adjust himself to the extraordinary requirements of the ordered self-control a king must have if it means a complete break with the side of life represented by Falstaff?

Question: How does the figure of "counterfeiting" enter into the total meaning of the play?

Answer: Counterfeiting, of course, is the subject of Falstaff's soliloquy on the battlefield when he rises up after playing possum to escape Douglas' sword. He has counterfeited death to escape death, and in these terms is no worse than the King, whose "counterfeits" (knights in his livery) have been cropping up like "Hydra's heads" on the field. The point is that Henry has been doing a good deal of counterfeiting all along in his dealings with the Percies, not to mention the fact that he is still, until his sway is irrevocably established, something of a "counterfeit" king, and is thus himself partially responsible for the disordered kingdom. Falstaff's speech, because he is absolutely without hypocrisy, is an ironic commentary on the deceptions the "nobles" practice on themselves and others. Even the Prince has been counterfeiting, in pretending to be wholeheartedly committed to Falstaff's way of life. Of course, all deception, for whatever end, can be regarded as a form of counterfeiting; even the thievery of Bardolph and the others thus comes under this heading. The important thing is that the dramatist localizes the various deceptions in the single idea of "counterfeiting" so that their analogous nature (with the **irony** this entails) is heavily underlined.

Question: What evidence is there to suggest that the Prince has never wholeheartedly given himself over to riot and dishonor?

Answer: The Prince has a certain scorn for Falstaff's way of life, which shows through even his most affectionate utterances. He never takes a spirited part in the robbery, and he later arranges to have the money repaid. In his early soliloquy, and later (in the "Francis" scene) we find his behavior associated with the "humors." This suggests that his is a transient inexplicable lapse from virtuous behavior-he is, in short, simply "not himself," as he makes clear in his interview with the King.

Furthermore, he treats the sheriff and the commoners generally (except for Francis) courteously. His decision to take up his rightful duties in the battle is so ready and unhesitating, and his gracious comments about Hotspur so frankly offered, that it is hard to think of Hal as a reformed prodigal. He has, in fact, the attitude of the good man temporarily fascinated or bewitched by some magic (just as Falstaff, facetiously, claims to have been given medicines by Poins to make him love him).

Question: What is significance of the events in the final scene of the play?

Answer: The opening lines of the scene, "Thus ever did rebellion find rebuke," establish, in the regular rhythm and the **alliteration** and symmetry of "rebellion find rebuke," the rounded finality of the action. Similarly, the final **couplet** ("And since this business so fair is done, / Let us not leave till all our own be won,"), in fact, Henry's entire closing speech, indicates the firmness and control of the King. What is more, the apparent arbitrariness of dispatching Worcester and Vernon to their deaths, while allowing Douglas his life, suggests that the power of regal decision-above question and petty motive-is being reaffirmed. Furthermore, the Prince's generosity toward Douglas (in freeing him) and toward Prince John (in allowing him the honor of delivering Douglas up), a generosity which has already been anticipated in his willingness to let Falstaff claim the "honor" of Percy's death, is one way of demonstrating that the air has finally been cleared of spite and jealousy.

BIBLIOGRAPHY AND GUIDE TO RESEARCH PAPERS

EDITIONS

Any advanced scholarly study of *Henry IV*, Part One must make considerable use of the volume *Henry the Fourth*, Part One (edited by S. B. Hemingway, 1936), in the *New Variorum Edition of Shakespeare*. The edition by John Dover Wilson (1946), however, is very useful for its authoritative introduction and pertinent notes. A helpful and compact students' edition, which contains the text of the play with useful footnotes, the texts of the principal sources for the play, and a copious and representative sampling of criticism-classical and modern-is *William Shakespeare: Henry the Fourth*, Part 1, edited by James L. Sanderson (New York: Norton Critical Editions, 1962).

Further Readings on Shakespeare and on Henry IV

Part One

Baldwin, T., Shakespeare's Five-Act Structure (1948).

Barber, C. L. *Shakespeare's Festive Comedy* (1959), Ch. 8, "Rule and Missrule in Henry IV."

Brandes, Georg, *Shakespeare* (1927): more a curiosity than a reliable guide, but makes some interesting points.

Brooks and Heilman, *Understanding Drama* (1945), Part Three, Sect. 4, "Shakespeare."

Bullough, Geoffrey, (ed.), Narrative and Dramatic Sources of Shakespeare, Vol. IV (1962).

Chambers, E. K., *Shakespeare: A Survey* (1925).

Charlton, H. B., *Shakespearean Comedy* (1938).

Coleridge, S. T., Coleridge's Shakespearean Criticism (1930).

Empson, William, *Some Versions of Pastoral* (1935).

Granville-Barker, Harley, Prefaces to Shakespeare (1946).

Hazlitt, William, Characters of Shakespeare's Plays (1870).

Holzknecht, Karl J., The Backgrounds of Shakespeare's Plays (1950).

Joseph, Sister Miriam, Shakespeare's Use of the Arts of Language (1946).

Morgann, Maurice, Essay on the Dramatic Character of Sir John Falstaff (1777), ed. W. A. Gill (1912).

Spurgeon, Caroline, *Shakespeare's **Imagery*** (1935).

Tillyard, E. M. W., *Shakespeare's History Plays* (1944).

Van Doren, Mark, *Shakespeare* (1953).

Wilson, John Dover, *The Fortunes of Falstaff* (1944).

Suggested Research Papers

1. Shakespeare's use of sources in *Henry IV*, Part One.

    See:

    a. Bullough, *Sources*.

    b. The Variorum Edition.

    Read the original sources for the play; study the alterations Shakespeare made in them - the shaping art he used in adapting them. What, for example, has he added to the character of Glendower as it appeared in the chronicle? How has he modified the idea of the Prince's waywardness? Write a paper analyzing in detail his handling of one (or more) of the sources.

2. **Imagery** as a contribution to the meaning of the play.

    See:

    a. Spurgeon, *Shakespeare's Imagery*.

    b. Downer, "The Life of Our Design."

    c. Brooks, "The Naked Babe."

    Select what appears to be a dominant image in the play (the image of disease or sickness, for example) and try to define as accurately as possible the contribution this makes to the total meaning. Or analyze the image-complex which results from the repetition of related images, for example, "crowns" and "heads."

3. The function of the double plot.

   See:

   a. Empson, *Versions of Pastoral*.

   b. Brooks and Heilman, *Understanding Drama*.

   c. Fergusson, *Idea of a Theatre*.

   Try to analyze the relationship between the main plot and the subplot. Is it one of analogy? Contrast? At what points in the action do the two plots merge? What characters are common to both? What proportion of the action is allotted to each? Where do the sharpest juxtapositions occur?

4. The dramatic importance of farcical scenes (this is of course related to the double plot idea).

   See:

   a. Empson, *Versions of Pastoral*.

   b. Kitto, *Form and Meaning*.

   c. Baldwin, *Five-Act Structure*.

   Consider in detail such scenes as the Prince-Francis jest, or the Gadshill-Carriers-Chamberlain **episode**. Do these have a function beyond humor for its own sake? Is there any "nonsense" which is truly without meaning, or are there parallels to be discovered with events or characters in the main plot? How do they help to create a sense of passing time?

5. The various **themes** of the play as related to a background of contemporary ethical, political, or philosophical thought.

See:

a. Tillyard, *World Picture.*

b. Campbell, *Shakespeare's "Histories."*

c. Allen, *Star-Crossed Renaissance.*

How seriously do **metaphors** suggesting a sympathetic correspondence among individuals, society, the earth, the universe, reflect Elizabethan beliefs? Note particularly Henry's opening speech (Act I, Scene 1) and his condemnation of Worcester (Act V, Scene 1) as an "exhaled meteor." In what ways do the political realities of the play touch on contemporary political life? To what extent does the play mirror the ideal of the "Renaissance prince?" It has been suggested that there is a leading ethical idea in the play which closely resembles the "golden mean" taught in Aristotle's *Nichomachean Ethics.* What evidence is there for this view?

6. The dramatic importance of special "languages" in the play.

See:

a. Downer, "Life of Our Design."

b. Empson, *Complex Words*.

c. Brooks, "Naked Babe."

d. Brooks and Heilman, *Understanding Drama*.

What does Falstaff's use of the Euphuistic" style (in his mock interview with the Prince) really amount to for the meaning of the play as a whole? What can be said about Falstaff's constant use of biblical phrases? His echoing of Puritan clichés? (See the *Variorum Edition* for the biblical identifications.) Are there any clear analogies between situations in the play and the biblical contexts his phrases suggest (for example, "Watch tonight, pray to-morrow")? what about Hotspur's "martial" vocabulary? the "language of love" spoken by Mortimer and his wife? her Welsh? the thieves' jargon spoken by Gadshill? Francis' almost total lack of language? How are these all related to images of speech, like Hotspur's "filling the mouth of deep defiance up"? or his reference to abandoning speech in favor of action? In general, what is the relation between language and action in the play?

7. An analysis of important puns and multileveled images.

   See:

   a. Empson, *Complex Words.*

   b. Empson, *Versions of Pastoral.*

   c. Spurgeon, *Shakespeare's Imagery.*

   d. Above all, *the Oxford English Dictionary.*

   e. Empson's *Seven Types of Ambiguity* might be of use.

   Follow one (or several) leading words through the play. (Examples: "crown," "head," "counterfeit," "honor," "courtesy," "neck," "current," "opinion," or "humor'" - there are many more which could profitably be studied.) What alternative meanings do they have? In what contexts is the potential fullness of meaning realized? When are they used (and by whom) in a restricted sense? How do they help to define character? to embody the major **themes** of the play?

8. Shakespeare's handling of plot.

   See:

   a. Baldwin, *Five-Act Structure.*

   b. Kitto, *Form and Meaning.*

   c. Fergusson, *Idea of a Theatre.*

How does the dramatist arrange the details of his story and with what results? (This might be better restricted to a single act or a single scene). How does <u>Act I</u> function as **exposition**? What else does it accomplish? How does Shakespeare suggest the passage of time? What is the dramatic function of such baffling scenes as <u>Act II, Scene 1</u> or <u>Act IV, Scene 4</u>? What is accomplished by the lengthy development of such **episodes** as Hotspur's chiding of Glendower (<u>Act III, Scene 1</u>)?

9. The relationship of style and meaning. The use of verse and prose, and the varying quality of the verse spoken by different characters, or by the same character at different times. (This might include an analysis of the figures of speech used by one or more of the players.)

See:

a. Granville-Barker, *On Dramatic Method.*

b. Sister Miriam Joseph, *Arts of Language.*

c. Auerbach, *Mimesis.*

Which characters always speak in verse? Which in prose? What does this mean? Analyze the long speeches of the King, Percy, the Prince, Worcester. How does the "quality" of speech (kind of **metaphor**, rhythm, density of language, tone) help to define the character? Can the degeneration of a character be seen as a difference in the way he speaks earlier and later? What is the importance of the "mystical" prattle of Glendower? the "poeticism" of Percy? How many times does Falstaff mimic the speech habits of another character? With what effect? How do

imagery and rhythm suggest action which cannot be represented on stage?

10. The most important question - the meaning of the play.

    See:

    a. Fergusson, *Idea of a Theatre*.

    b. Fergusson, *Human Image ("Macbeth")*.

    c. Barber, *Festive Comedy*.

    d. Kitto, *Form and Meaning*.

    What is the plot center? Of what "action" is *Henry IV Part One* an imitation?

    The play is a vast complex arrangement of analogous actions, speeches, deceptions, rationalizations, and many other details. What underlying "action" (see "Appendix" in *Fergusson's Idea of a Theatre*) do all the characters mirror in their own special ways?

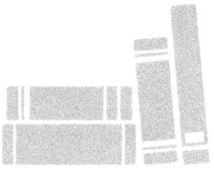

HENRY IV, PART 1

GENERAL BIOGRAPHY AND CRITICISM

Alexander, P., *Shakespeare's Life and Art*, New York, 1961. Development of Shakespeare from apprentice to mature artist.

Brooks, C., "Shakespeare as a symbolist poet," *Yale Rev.*, June, 1945.

Chambers, E. K., *The Elizabethan Stage*, Oxford, 1923. A classic for the study of Shakespeare's stage problems.

Coleridge, S. T., *Shakespearean Criticism*, reprint, New York, 1961. An interesting study of the play from a nineteenth century critic's viewpoint.

Farnham, Willard, *Medieval Heritage of Elizabethan Tragedy*, New York, 1956. One of the most complete studies of the classical vs. medieval concept of tragedy. Excellent comments on *King Richard III*.

Goddard, Harold, *The Meaning of Shakespeare*, New York.

Green, V. H. H., *The Later Plantagenets*, London, 1955. Shows the weakness of the line that accounts for their fall from power.

Hazlitt, Wm., *Characters of Shakespeare's Plays*, modern reprint. Thinks *King Richard III* is better on the stage than read in quiet, as was then being urged by some.

Hughes, A. E., *Shakespeare and His Welsh Characters*. Interesting comments on the Duke of Richmond and his Welsh background.

Perry, Alice I., *Stage History of Shakespeare's King Richard The Third*, New York, 1909. This work gives a full account of the various acting editions of the play.

Rowse, A. L., *William Shakespeare*, New York, 1963. Gives an excellent re-evaluation of the critics' views on *King Richard III*.

Sprague, A. C., *Shakespearean Players and Performances*, Cambridge, 1954. An account of the late sixteenth century stage.

GENERAL: CLASSIC CRITICISM AND INTERPRETATION

Bradley, A. C. "Shakespeare's *Antony and Cleopatra*" in *Oxford Lectures on Poetry*. London, 1950.

Case, R. H. and M. R. Ridley. Introduction to the Arden edition of Antony and Cleopatra. Cambridge, Mass., 1955.

Chambers, E. K. *Shakespeare: A Survey*. London, 1925.

Charney, Maurice. *Shakespeare's Roman Plays*. Cambridge, Mass., 1961.

Coleridge, S. T. *Notes and Lectures upon Shakespeare*. London, 1849, V. I, 145-148.

Danby, John F. *Poets on Fortune's Hill*. London, 1952.

Dickey, Franklin M. *Not Wisely, But Too Well.* San Marino, Calif., 1957.

Dowden, Edward. *Shakespeare.* N. Y., 1881.

Dryden, John. Preface to All for Love in Mermaid Series. London, 1949-50

Farnham, Willard. *Shakespeare's Tragic Frontier.* Berkeley, Calif., 1950.

Granville-Barker, Harley. *Prefaces to Shakespeare.* Princeton, N. J., 1952, V. I.

Hazlitt, William. *Characters of Shakespeare's Plays.* London, 1957.

Holzknecht, Karl J. The Background of Shakespeare's Plays. N. Y., 1950.

Johnson, Samuel. *Samuel Johnson on Shakespeare* (ed. W. K. Wimsatt, Jr.). N. Y., 1960.

Knight, G. Wilson. *The Imperial **Theme**.* London, 1951.

Knights, Lionel C. *Some Shakespearean Themes.* Stanford, Calif., 1960.

Mac Callum, M. W. *Shakespeare's Roman Plays.* London, 1910.

Mack, Maynard. Introduction to the Pelican edition of Antony and Cleopatra. Baltimore, 1960.

Ribner, Irving. Patterns in Shakespearean Tragedy. N. Y., 1960.

Rosen, William. *Shakespeare and the Craft of Tragedy.* Cambridge, Mass., 1960.

Spencer, T. J. B. *Shakespeare: The Roman Plays.* London, 1963.

Spurgeon, Caroline. *Shakespeare's **Imagery**.* Boston, 1958.

Symons, Arthur. "Antony and Cleopatra," in *Studies in the Elizabethan Drama.* London, 1920.

Traversi, D. A. *Approach to Shakespeare.* London, 1938.

Van Doren, Mark. *Shakespeare*, N. Y., 1939.

Wilson, Harold S. On the Design of Shakespearean Tragedy. Toronto, 1957.

Readings In Critical Methods as Applied to Shakespeare

Auerbach, Erich, *Mimesis* (1953), Ch. 13, "The Weary Prince" (Prince Hal in *Henry IV, Part Two*).

Brooks, Cleanth, *The Well-Wrought Urn* (1947), Ch. 2, "The Naked Babe and the Cloak of Manliness," (a study of **imagery** in *Macbeth).*

Downer, Alan S., "The Life of Our Design: The Function of **Imagery** in the Poetic Drama," in *Shakespeare: Modern Essays in Criticism*, ed. Leonard Dean (1957).

Empson, William, *The Structure of Complex Words* (1951), chapters on "Fool in *Lear,*" and "Honest in *Othello."*

Fergusson, Francis, *The Human Image in Dramatic Literature* (1957), Part II, "Shakespeare."

____*The Idea of a Theatre* (1949), Ch. 4, "'*Hamlet,* Prince of Denmark;' The Analogy of Action."

Granville-Barker, Harley *On Dramatic Method* (1956), Ch. 3, "Shakespeare's Progress."

Kitto, H. D. F., *Form and Meaning in Drama* (1956), Ch. 9 *"Hamlet."*

LIFE AND TIMES OF SHAKESPEARE

Chute, Marchette. *Shakespeare of London*. New York, 1956. A very interesting biography that also provides analysis of Shakespeare's world.

Halliday, F. E. *Shakespeare: A Pictorial Biography*. New York, 1956. Excellent pictures.

Fluchere, Henri. *Shakespeare and the Elizabethans*. New York, 1956. Relates Shakespeare to the other dramatists of his time and to the world in which they lived.

Spencer, Theodore. *Shakespeare and the Nature of Men*. New York, 1951. A discussion of the philosophical background of Shakespeare's England with particular emphasis on man's place in nature.

Trevelyan, G. M. *History of England, Volume II: The Tudors and the Stuart Era*. New York, 1953. A good account of the history of Tudor England.

Tillyard, E. M. *The Elizabethan World Picture*. New York, 1944. An excellent description of the concepts, attitudes, and manners in Shakespearean England, supplying important background material for the understanding of all Shakespeare's work.

SHAKESPEAREAN THEATER PRODUCTION

Adams, John Cranford. The Globe Playhouse: Its Design and Equipment. New York, 1942.

De Banke, Cecile. Shakespearean Production, Then and Now. A Manual for the Scholar Player. New York, 1953.

Hodges, C. Walter. *The Globe Restored*. New York, 1954.

Smith, Irwin. Shakespeare's Globe Playhouse. A Modern Reconstruction in Text and Scale Drawings. New York, 1956.

These books describe the ways in which Shakespeare's plays were originally produced, and De Banke's account includes helpful suggestions for the modern producer.

SHAKESPEARE'S HISTORY PLAYS

Campbell, Lily B. *Shakespeare's Histories: Mirrors of Elizabethan Policy*. San Marino, California, 1947. An excellent description of the development of historiography in the English Renaissance, with a separate chapter on *Henry V* analyzed as the ideal victorious king.

Chambers E. K. *Shakespeares A Survey*. New York, 1959. A collection of essays on various Shakespeare plays, including an excellent chapter on *Henry V* in relation to patriotism in sixteenth century England.

Holzknecht, Karl J. *The Backgrounds of Shakespeare's Plays*. New York, 1950. A particularly useful account of the role of chroniclers and writers of popular history works for the theater in Tudor England. Shakespeare is seen in perspective with other men also concerned with historical themes.

Schelling, R. E. *The English Chronicle Play*. New York, 1902. An interesting discussion of the **genre** of the chronicle play flourishing before and during Shakespeare's lifetime.

Tillyard, E. M. W. *Shakespeare's History Plays*. London, 1956. An analysis of the myth of the Tudor Monarchy and the men who celebrated it in chronicle and drama, including Shakespeare. There is an excellent chapter on *Henry V* in this connection.

Traversi, Derek. *From Richard II to Henry V* Stanford, California, 1957. An exploration of the dominant **themes** in Shakespeare's **epic** of English history, with an interesting chapter emphasizing the moral development of the character of Henry V.

www.ingramcontent.com/pod-product-compliance
Lightning Source LLC
LaVergne TN
LVHW011714060526
838200LV00051B/2898